P9-EMF-576

ASTHMA

ASTHMA

by Alissa Greenberg, M.D.

Franklin Watts
A Division of Grolier Publishing
New York • London • Hong Kong • Sydney
Danbury, Connecticut

Note to readers: Words in **bold** are defined in the glossary.

Photographs ©: Anatomyworks: 21 (John Hagen), 18; Archive Photos: 10, 99 (Gary Hershorn/Reuters); Corbis-Bettmann: 22 (Lester V. Bergman), 36 (Janet Wishnetsky), 14, 15; Medichrome/StockShop: 48 (Paul Bowling), 83 (Jon Riley), 53 (Michael Tamborrino); Photo Researchers: chapter headers, cover, 1, 9 background (Gary Carlson), 90 (Mark Clarke/SPL), 33 (Eddy Gray/SPL), 28 (Carlyn Iverson), 71, 92 (Damien Lovegrove/SPL), 88 (Will & Deni McIntyre), 58 (Oliver Meckes), 70 (Gregory K. Scott); PhotoEdit: 79 (Amy C. Etra), 107 (Michael Newman), 63 (Mary M. Steinbacher); Stock Boston: 86 (Laima Druskis), 102 (Judy S. Gelles), 43 (Stacy Pick); Visuals Unlimited: 25 (David M. Phillips), 54 (SIU).

Interior design by A. Natacha Pimentel C.

Visit Franklin Watts on the Internet at:

http://publishing.grolier.com

Library of Congress Cataloging-in-Publication Data

Greenberg, Alissa.
   Asthma / Alissa Greenberg.
     p. cm.
   Includes bibliographical references and index.
   Summary: Describes the symptoms, causes, diagnosis, and treatment of asthma, as well as guidelines for living with the disease.
   ISBN 0-531-11331-0
   1. Asthma—Juvenile literature. [1. Asthma. 2. Diseases.] I. Title.

RC591.G74 2000
616.2'38—dc21   99-086993

© 2000 by Alissa Greenberg
All rights reserved. Published simultaneously in Canada.
Printed in the United States of America.
1 2 3 4 5 6 7 8 9 10 R 09 08 07 06 05 04 03 02 01 00

GROLIER
PUBLISHING

To my family

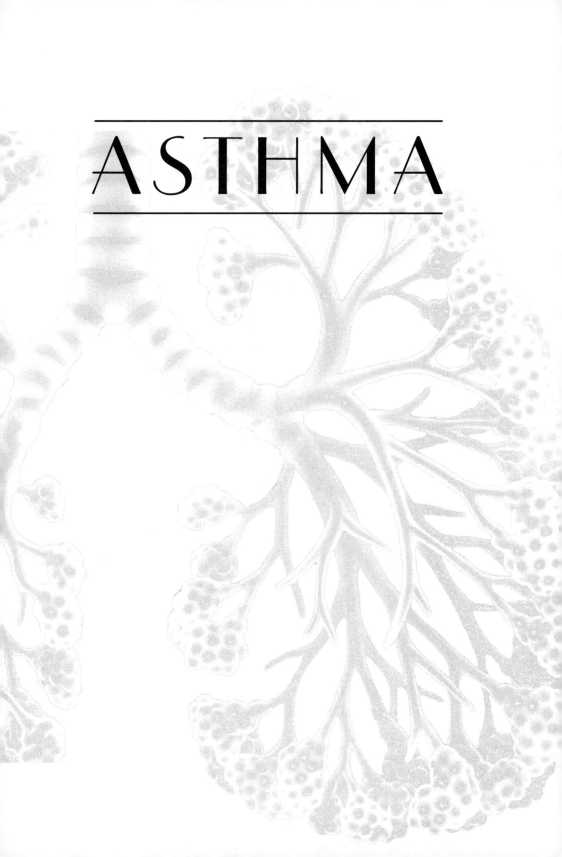

ASTHMA

Tom Dolan, a swimmer with asthma, raises his hands after winning a gold medal at the 1996 Olympic Games.

Tom Dolan was streaking through the water. He was sure he would achieve his goal and become the first American to win a gold medal at the 1996 Olympic Games in Atlanta, Georgia. But as the swimmer began his last lap, he felt his airways tighten—a warning sign of an **asthma** attack. He later explained, "I really couldn't get any oxygen at all. . . . But I knew there was 50 meters to go to get a gold medal. That's all there was to it." Yet by the time he climbed out of the pool, victorious, he recalled, "I don't know whether it was the adrenaline rush of winning or what. . . . All I know is my asthma wasn't bothering me at all."[1]

Tom Dolan has suffered from asthma since he was twelve years old, but it never stopped him from doing whatever he wanted to do. "My doctors told me I had pretty severe asthma, but this was not going to interfere with me attaining my goals. . . . I don't really think about my asthma that much, except that I have to take my medications regularly."[2]

The treatment of asthma has changed a lot in recent years. Children with asthma used to be kept indoors when they started to wheeze, and Olympic competition was considered unrealistic. But now the goals of treatment are to help people with asthma live normal—and possibly extraordinary—lives.

CHAPTER 1

What Is Asthma?

The word *asthma* comes from the ancient Greek verb *aazein*, meaning "to breathe with an open mouth" or "to pant." As the name suggests, asthma is a condition that affects our natural ability to breathe.

A Brief History of Asthma

Asthma has been recognized as a distinct illness for at least 2,000 years and perhaps more than 4,000. Yet we still have many questions about the causes and processes of asthma, and a cure has not yet been found.

The first written description of an asthma attack comes from ancient China. The *Nei Ching*, written by Huang Ti, "the Yellow Emperor" (2698–2598 B.C.), is considered the oldest book of internal medicine. In this book, Huang Ti recorded a conversation with one of his ministers about a condition of troubled, noisy breathing: "Man is afflicted he cannot rest and when his breathing has a sound."[1] According to the ancient Chinese, the disease was due to an imbalance of the yin and yang—two principles of nature that make up all things. The treatment was usually acupuncture, a technique that uses long thin needles to stimulate specific points on the body and bring the yin and yang back into balance. Acupuncture is still used today to treat many diseases, including asthma. The *Nei Ching* also mentions the use of a plant called *ma huang*. This plant has been found to contain a chemical called ephedrine, which is still used in the treatment of acute asthma attacks.

Artifacts from ancient Egypt suggest that asthma was identified even earlier. Respiratory problems among the workers who built the pyramids may have been the first cases of occupational asthma—asthma caused by something in the work environment. A papyrus written in 1550 B.C. seems to compile medical texts dating as far back as 3000 B.C. One disease described in this document is a condition of noisy, difficult breathing that may have been asthma. The text lists many possible treatments, including the use of camel and crocodile body waste, inhalation of various herbs, and enemas (the injection of liquid into the intestine through the anus).[2]

The term *asthma* first appeared in the *Corpus Hippocratum,* a work edited by the ancient Greek physician Hippocrates (460–380 B.C.). (Hippocrates gave us the Hippocratic oath, which is a code of medical ethics usually taken by new doctors.) In this work and in later Greek and Roman writings, the disease is defined as panting or troubled breathing not associated with fever. Hippocrates thought asthma was the result of an imbalance of humors, or liquids in the body, leading to a flow of evil phlegm, or mucus, from the brain down into the lungs. The treatment was to encourage the flow of the phlegm by inducing vomiting, excretion, or bleeding.[3]

Hippocrates, at the bedside of a sick youth, was the first physician to define asthma.

Another Greek physician, Aretaeus (A.D. 81–131), provided a description of asthma that still applies today: "The symptoms of its approach are a heaviness of the chest, sluggishness to one's accustomed work and to every other exertion, difficulty in breathing on a steep road. . . . But if the evil gradually gets worse, a wheeze during the waking state, but the evil much worse in sleep, a desire of much and of cold air . . . they breathe standing as if desiring to draw all the air which they can possibly inhale and they also open the mouth."[4]

The ancient Romans based most of their medicine on Greek knowledge and developed a treatment called "similitude," or using like to treat like. For example, they recommended eating the lungs of foxes as a cure for asthma.

After the decline and fall of the Roman Empire in the fifth century A.D., the Western world entered the so-called Dark Ages, and there was little progress in medicine. However, one physician during this time wrote a work on asthma that contains advice doctors still use today. Moses Maimonides (1135–1204), physician to the Egyptian sultan of Saladin, wrote a *Treatise on Asthma* for Saladin's son with asthma. Maimonides stressed the need for individual treatments for every person with asthma. He warned against emotional turmoil or stress and recommended that the prince move to Cairo, where the air was dry. He also mentioned hot chicken soup as a possible remedy.[5] These recommendations are similar to some current treatments for asthma.

Maimonides believed that each case of asthma required individual treatment. Some of his advice is still used today.

Not until the 1600s did scientists make any real advances in understanding the causes of asthma, however. By then, the disease was described as fits or seizures of the lungs during which the airways draw together and become narrow. Some physicians recognized underlying causes of the disease, including heredity, weather, seasons, pollution, tobacco smoke, infection, exercise, and emotions. They were getting close to the current understanding of the cause of asthma attacks.

However, physicians seemed to be moving backwards in their treatments of asthma. One popular treatment was the use of horse dung, reminiscent of the ancient Egyptians' use of crocodile and camel body waste. Another common prescription was to eat fox lung, like the ancient Romans did. Many people were convinced that smoking tobacco could relieve asthma. We now know that tobacco smoke is one of the worst culprits in bringing on asthma attacks and may even play a role in the development of asthma.

In the 1800s, new technologies enabled researchers to finally identify some of the cells involved in causing asthma. And in the beginning of the 1900s, the term **allergy** was coined. The word is derived from the Greek *allos,* meaning "other," and indicated an abnormal reaction to a substance foreign to the body. Along with a clearer understanding of the mechanisms of asthma, more effective treatments were developed. However, many treatments were given as inhalants in combination with tobacco, thus destroying any possible benefits.

In the second half of the twentieth century, we made important strides in our understanding of asthma. We now understand the workings of the **pulmonary** system and immune system and know that they interact to cause asthma. Asthma treatment has progressed from being reactive—treating attacks after they occur—to being proactive—trying to prevent attacks altogether.

Definitions of Asthma

Although asthma has been recognized as a disease for a very long time, definitions of asthma have changed over the years. Until recently, asthma was thought to be an episodic condition in which attacks or episodes occurred from time to time. We now know that it is actually a chronic condition, meaning it is always present. People with asthma experience periods during which they cannot get enough air because the tubes carrying air from the nose and mouth into the body are abnormal and tend to become narrowed. Attacks vary from a mild feeling of tightness in the chest or a cough to severe shortness of breath. The episodes can last minutes, hours, or days and may fade on their own or with medication.

Although people with asthma may breathe normally between attacks, this does not mean they are free of the disease. In people with asthma, the air passages that carry air from the nose or mouth to the lungs are abnormal. These airways are always swollen and irritated or inflamed. Air can still pass through the airways, but when they are exposed to certain "triggers," or irritants, they may narrow to the point where air can no longer pass through them freely. The airways are called **hyperresponsive** or **hyperreactive** because of this tendency to constrict when irritated. Asthma is also sometimes called "reactive airway disease."

When the airways constrict, the person becomes short of breath. The air passing through these narrow airways often makes a high-pitched sound called **wheezing**, which can be audible to other people. The **inflammation** of the airways

17

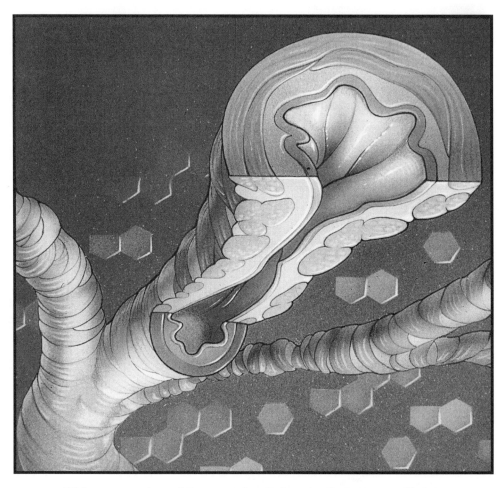

This cross section of the constricted airway of a person suffering from asthma shows an abnormally thickened bronchial wall and a narrowed air passage.

causes increased mucus production, which makes many people cough. The mucus sometimes builds up and plugs the airways, causing even more shortness of breath.

Although people with asthma may have no symptoms between attacks, the fear of an attack can affect the way they live. The body requires several basic elements to survive—

food, water, and air. A person can live more than a month without food, about a week without water, but only about five minutes without air. If you try to hold your breath, you know it is hard to hold it for more than one minute. If you try to hold it much longer, you will pass out and then your breathing will start automatically. The body prevents you from suffocating in this way. So asthma affects one of the body's most basic needs.

An asthma attack can be a frightening experience. If you do not have asthma and want to know what an attack might feel like, try running up a flight of stairs breathing only through a straw in your mouth—you may have to pinch your nose closed while you do this. (Do not try this if you have asthma or any other disease of the lungs or heart.) Now imagine that you cannot remove the straw and that you have to walk, climb stairs, or run breathing only through a straw.

CHAPTER 2

What Causes Asthma?

Asthma is caused by an interaction between the pulmonary system and the immune system. In order to understand the cause of this disease, you need to know something about these two body systems.

The Pulmonary System

Human beings and other members of the animal kingdom are aerobes, which means we need oxygen to survive. Creatures who do not need oxygen—some types of bacteria, for example—are called anaerobes. Every cell in the human body needs to get energy from oxygen to do its job. The pulmonary system brings the oxygen into the body and to all the cells, and it disposes of the carbon dioxide waste produced by the cells.

Air enters the body through the nose and mouth, then travels to a large tube called the trachea. The trachea goes down through chest and divides into two branches—airways called the right and left main **bronchi**. The bronchi then divide into smaller and smaller branches, forming the right and left lungs.

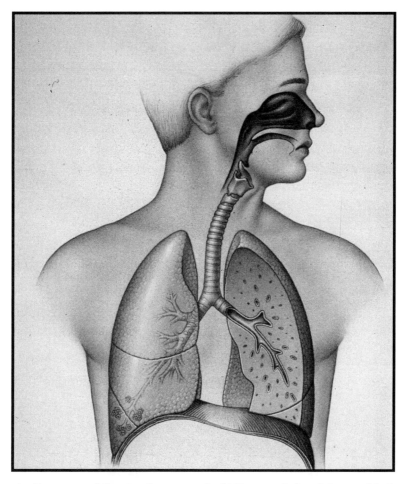

A diagram of the trachea, or windpipe, and the right and left main bronchi of the human lungs

These branching airways are called the tracheo-bronchial tree. The surface area of the bronchial tree and the lungs comes into close contact with blood vessels. The smallest and last branches of the airways divide into thousands of **alveoli**, or small sacs, where air is in close contact with thin-walled blood vessels called capillaries. Here the oxygen travels through the thin porous walls of the alveoli into the blood carried by the capillaries. The blood, now rich in oxygen, travels to the left side of the heart and is pumped through the circulatory system to every cell in the body.

One very important function of the lung is to protect the body from the harmful substances we inhale every time we take a breath. The lungs protect the body from these substances with the help of the immune system.

Agents of Disease

We are surrounded by disease-causing organisms and agents. Some are microscopic creatures and some are nonliving particles of dust or pollution.

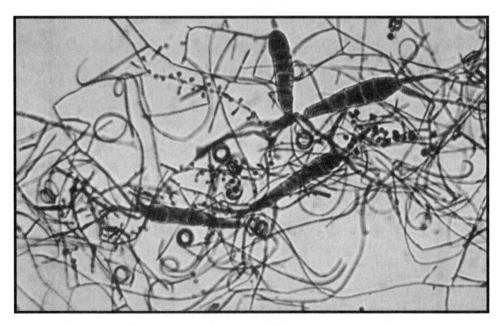

Fungi are disease-causing agents. This fungus, seen through a microscope, causes athlete's foot in humans.

The living disease-causing agents are bacteria, viruses, and fungi. They are also called **pathogens**, from a Latin word meaning "to cause suffering."

Bacteria are single-celled organisms that can enter the body. If they are not stopped, they can multiply rapidly and may cause disease by releasing toxins or poisons in the body.

Viruses are so small that they can be seen only with specialized electron microscopes. Viruses cannot live on their own. They require host cells to survive. When viruses enter a body, they move into the cells of that body—the host—and take over. They use the host cells to reproduce themselves rapidly, and the viruses they produce then invade more host cells. So viruses cause disease—by preventing the host cells from doing their job, or by killing the host cells.

Fungi include mushrooms, molds, and yeast. Some are microscopic, while others grow big enough to be seen by the naked eye. Fungi are made up of cells similar to plant cells, but they lack chlorophyll—the substance that makes plants green. When fungi enter the body they may reproduce so abundantly that they interfere with the normal functioning of the host cells, causing disease. They can also trigger an abnormal response by the immune system. This ability has special significance in asthma.

Nonliving agents can also cause disease if they get into the body. For example, some substances are know to be cancer-causing.

Some substances in our environment are not usually harmful, but they can cause disease in people whose immune system reacts inappropriately. Asthma may be caused this way, as you will see in later chapters of this book.

The Immune System

So we are surrounded by agents that can cause disease: bacteria, viruses, fungi, dust, pollution, and others. How are people able to survive? The immune (from the Latin word *immunis,* meaning "exempt") system protects us from pathogens. With the many defense mechanisms of the immune system, the body becomes a virtual fortress. It has a moat, barricades, an alarm system, sentries, dogs, and a well-equipped, highly sophisticated army to defend it.

Barricades and Moats

The body's first line of defense is physical. A thick layer of skin covering most of the body forms an effective barrier. In addition, glands in the skin produce an oily secretion called sebum, which is acidic and kills most bacteria.

A thinner mucous membrane covers the inside surfaces of the body—the gastrointestinal tract, the genital and urinary tracts, and the respiratory tract. This membrane is weaker, but it has other mechanisms to protect it. Saliva, tears, and mucus wash away potential invaders. Thick mucus acts like glue and traps foreign organisms. Colonies of harmless resident microorganisms live on these membranes and compete with pathogens for places to attach on the surface. In some areas, such as the respiratory and gastrointestinal tracts, the mucous membrane is covered by **cilia**—hairlike projections—that move in waves to propel microorganisms out of the body. This defense mechanism is called the "mucocilliary escalator." Finally, chemicals and acids are secreted by some surfaces. For example, acid in the stomach kills most swallowed pathogens.

Breaks in the skin from cuts or scrapes can allow pathogens to enter the body. Biting insects can also

Cilia are tiny hairlike projections on the surface of cells that move in waves to sweep mucus and foreign particles out of the respiratory system.

introduce pathogens as they feed. For example, Lyme disease is spread by tick bites, fleabites can transmit bubonic plague, and when mosquitoes bite, they can deposit the protozoan that causes malaria.

Guard Dogs

But not to worry. If an invader breaches the barricades of the immune system, it faces other defense mechanisms. The guard dogs of the immune system form the next line of defense. Various cells patrol the body, ingesting foreign particles wherever they find them. Almost any cell can ingest small particles, but specialized **white blood cells** called **phagocytes** (from Greek words meaning "eating cells") can handle larger particles.

Alarm System

Besides the barricades and guard dogs, the body also has an alarm system. Damage to body tissue of almost any type sets off the release of a variety of chemicals that alerts the body that damage has occurred and that an invasion may be ready to take place. These chemicals stimulate a rapid and powerful response from the body in the area of the damage. First, the diameter of blood vessels increases, allowing increased blood flow to the damaged area. The increased blood flow brings many other cells into the area to help in the defensive action. The local blood vessels become leaky and fluids and cells leave the vessels and accumulate in the damaged area. The chemicals also attract large numbers of phagocytes. This process is called **chemotaxis**. The phagocytes ingest the invading pathogens, but they cause damage to host tissue as well. This damage releases more of the inflammatory chemicals and strengthens the response to the invaders.

Eventually, if the host succeeds in warding off an invasion, a substance called fibrin walls off the area, and the phagocytes clean up the battle debris. This rapid alarm and response produces the redness, swelling, and pain that you see after a cut or scrape. It is called inflammation.

The Army

If an invading pathogen is successful in getting by this set of defenses, the body has even more sophisticated methods of warding off invaders. The immune system has an army of cells that can recognize and selectively eliminate foreign agents. These cells are some of the many types of white blood cells or **leukocytes** produced in the bone marrow, which then circulate in the blood and reside in other tissues. Some of the most important members of this army are the **antigen presenting cells**, **B-lymphocytes**, **T-lymphocytes**, **eosinophils**, and **mast cells.**

Antigen Presenting Cells

Antigen presenting cells are the scouts of the immune system army. They are a group of several types of cells that travel in the blood and search for invaders. When they find a foreign particle, they ingest it, process it, and then display a portion of it on their cell surface so that other cells of the immune system can recognize it. Various cells can act as antigen presenting cells. They congregate in areas where pathogens are likely to invade—such as the skin, lungs, or gastrointestinal tract. Often they will then travel with the **antigen** to areas of the body where there are high concentrations of immune system cells, so they can present it to a large number at once.

B-lymphocytes

B-lymphocytes, or **B-cells**, form and mature within the bone marrow (thus the name B-lymphocytes, for bone marrow) and then directly enter the bloodstream. These cells circulate with the blood and collect in lymph glands in areas such as the armpits, groin, and neck.

The B-cells have weapons called **antibodies**. Antibodies

are proteins on the surface of B-cells that can recognize foreign pathogens. When a B-cell meets a foreign pathogen with a molecule on its cell surface (called an antigen) that matches its antibody, the B-cell is stimulated to divide and multiply—thus producing many B-cells with the same antibody. These cells can then rapidly produce and release large numbers of the antibody—more than

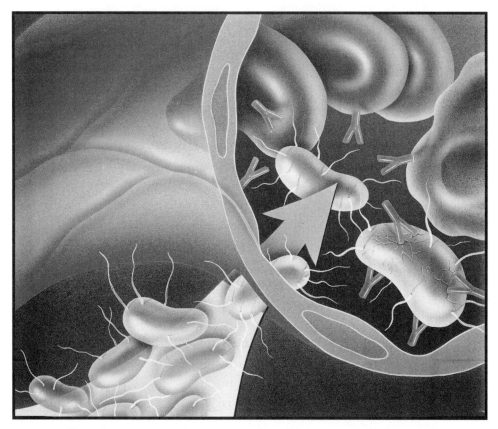

This diagram of the antigen/antibody reaction shows Y-shaped antibodies attaching to surface antigens on bacterial cells as the cells enter the bloodstream. The bacteria are the bean-shaped organisms with hairlike projections and the red cells are larger and oval shaped with indentations.

2,000 copies of the antibody per second. The antibodies bind to antigens on the foreign pathogen and mark the pathogen for destruction by other cells—such as phagocytes. The process is like spraying red paint on enemy invaders, so they become obvious targets for the other cells of the immune system army. Antibodies can also neutralize toxins or viral particles by coating them and preventing their binding to host cells.

When a B-cell meets a pathogen with an antigen matching its antibody, another type of B-cell called a memory B-cell is formed. These cells live for many years and continue to have the same antibody on their surface—thus preserving the memory for this antigen. So if the same enemy invades again, the immune system is ready for it. The memory B-cells can quickly divide and produce large amounts of antibodies, and the pathogen is rapidly killed. This is the reason many diseases cannot make a person sick twice. For example, if you have had chicken pox once you will not get it again. You are carrying antibodies ready to recognize and mark that virus for destruction.

T-lymphocytes

T-lymphocytes also begin their lives in the bone marrow, but they then migrate to the thymus gland located in the chest to mature (thus the name **T-cells**, for thymus). T-cells have structures on their cell surfaces called receptors. Like B-cells, T-cells circulate in the body, and when they meet appropriate antigens for their receptors, they divide and multiply into several different subtypes of T-cells.

The **cytotoxic** T-cells are the assassins of the immune system army. When activated, they release toxic substances that destroy cells that pathogens such as viruses have invaded. The helper T-cells act more like the generals of the army than like the lowly assistants their name implies. These cells direct the activity of the other immune system cells by releasing different signaling chemicals called **cytokines**. In the normal immune response, these cells release cytokines that activate the cytotoxic **lymphocytes**, phagocytes, and B-cells to identify and destroy the invading pathogen. As we shall see, if these generals give the wrong signals, the immune response goes awry, and this is perhaps how asthma develops.

Eosinophils and Mast Cells

Eosinophils and mast cells are specialized white blood cells, which when activated release chemicals called cytokines. These cytokines include histamine and **leukotrienes**, which, as we will see, play an important role in asthma and allergy. The role of these cells in the normal immune response is not clear. They do increase the inflammatory response, and they may play an important part in fighting off parasitic infections.

The Normal Immune Response in the Lungs

With all these forces of the immune system working together, the body is a well-defended fortress, and most of the time it is able to fend off or control invasions. However, this extremely powerful defense force can also cause disease if it malfunctions and damages the host body or overreacts to a substance that is not pathogenic.

The lungs are one of the primary battlegrounds in this constant struggle between invading pathogens and the body's defense forces. Whenever we take a breath we inhale a large number of particles in the air—including dust, pollution, pollen, bacteria, fungi, and viruses. The pulmonary system is well fortified to prevent illness caused by these billions of particles inhaled with every breath.

First, it has tough physical barriers to invasion. The nose filters out most particles over 5 micrometers (a micrometer is 1/1,000 of a meter). It also warms and humidifies air—protecting the lower airways from the irritating effect of dry, cold air. Smaller particles can penetrate to the lower airways, but if they land in the tracheobronchial tree, the mucocilliary escalator clears them out. Sneezing and coughing helps expel particles of all sizes. Particles that reach the alveoli are normally eaten by the resident guard dogs, the pulmonary **macrophages** (phagocytic cells that also act as antigen presenting cells). Then the mucocilliary escalator usually carries them out of the lungs.

If the invaders do get past the physical barriers, alarm system, and guard dogs of the immune system in the lungs, the scouts or antigen presenting cells find the pathogen and present it to lymphocytes. The generals, or helper T-cells, recognize the antigen and release cytokines to activate the army of B-cells, cytotoxic lymphocytes, phagocytes, and others. The B-cells release antibodies to mark the pathogens wherever they may have traveled. The cytotoxic lymphocytes and phagocytes destroy the invaders.

The Causes of Asthma

Asthma is probably caused by a malfunction of these immune mechanisms in the lungs. With a basic understanding of the pulmonary and immune systems and their interactions, we can explore the current theories about the causes of asthma. Although asthma has been recognized for many years, until recently the cause of the disease has

31

been a mystery. Advances in the study of immunology have led to some headway in understanding asthma.

Asthma is a chronic inflammatory disorder of the airways in which many cells and cell products of the immune system play a role. Inhaled irritants from the environment damage the airways and provoke inflammation. The inflammation causes airway swelling or edema, **bronchoconstriction** (spasms of the muscles surrounding the airways), and increased mucus production. These three things—edema, muscle spasm, and mucus—cause the air passages to become narrowed, leading to obstruction of airflow. When this occurs, the person experiences the symptoms of wheezing, breathlessness, chest tightness, and coughing.

But why do asthmatic lungs react to irritants in this way? One theory is that, in people with asthma, the immune mechanisms in the lungs do not function in a normal way. The first stage in the development of asthma may be a "sensitization" process during infancy or early childhood. People who are susceptible to the development of asthma, probably due to genetic factors, are exposed to an irritant, or **allergen**—usually an inhaled substance—such as cigarette smoke, dust, or animal **dander** (dried particles of skin or hair that float in the air). Antigen presenting cells pick up the irritant and present it to T-cells, as they should.

However, in people who are prone to develop asthma, something goes wrong. The helper T-cells produce a particular set of stimulatory chemicals different from those produced in the normal immune response. Helper T-cells that produce these particular cytokines are called **TH2** (type 2 helper) cells. These cytokines produce a cascade of responses. A cascade is something that happens in a series, one action leading to the next, inevitably progressing to the end. The asthma cascade is a series of events that build up to an asthma attack.

TH2 cells stimulate the B-cells to produce a particular type of antibody called **IgE**. Then both the cytokines released by TH2 cells and the IgE bind to various types of white blood cells, including mast cells, eosinophils and

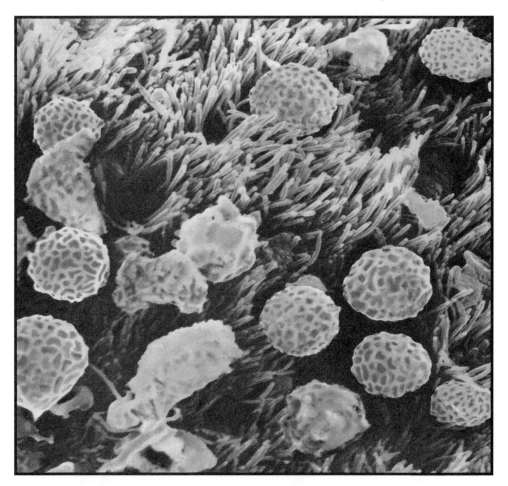

A microscopic view of the surface of the trachea covered in allergens, or irritants

macrophages, which are all abundant in the airways. These cells become activated and can release additional cytokines, which cause constriction of the muscle surrounding the airways (bronchoconstriction), and the airways become narrowed. They also damage the surrounding tissues and trigger the body's alarm system response—causing swelling of the airways and an influx of inflammatory cells. The inflammatory cells release more cytokines, which cause further bronchoconstriction, mucus production, and inflammation. So the cascade continues, building in intensity. Unless the cycle of inflammation can be broken, the airways remain swollen and narrowed and hyperreactive to further stimuli.

Even after the sensitizing irritant is gone, the airways are no longer normal. Repeated stimulation will cause long-term changes in the airways with thickening and scarring of the airway lining, growth of the muscle layer, growth and hyperactivity of the mucus glands, and an increased population of inflammatory cells that may stimulate bronchoconstriction when triggered.

An asthma attack caused by an irritant has two parts. At first, the person wheezes and coughs. This is caused by the irritant or allergen binding to the waiting IgE antibody, leading to immediate mast cell and eosinophil activation and the release of chemicals causing muscle contraction, mucus production, and airway swelling. The chemicals released during this initial phase attract inflammatory cells to the airways, and up to several days later, there may be continued inflammation and airway swelling, with continued wheezing and shortness of breath. The persistent inflammation makes the already sensitive airways even more irritable and hyperresponsive to any additional stimuli.

Who Gets Asthma and Why?

CHAPTER 3

Asthma is a common disease. About 100 million people worldwide suffer from asthma, and some 40,000 people die of this disease every year. In the United States more than 15 million people, including almost 3.7 million children, have asthma. It is now the most common chronic disease of childhood.[1]

These numbers reflect a huge increase in the **incidence** of asthma worldwide. In some areas, the incidence has increased by more than 100 percent over the last ten years. In the United States, the incidence of asthma increased 60 percent from 1986 to 1996. Some of this increase may be due to better diagnosis, improved access to health care, more careful reporting by physicians, or other factors. However, studies in many countries have consistently shown an increasing incidence of asthma. The reason for the increase is not clear, but there are many theories.[2]

In most of the world the increase of asthma is primarily in more affluent groups. But in the United States, the highest increases are in the inner cities and among minority groups. The rates for African-American men are rising at

Children suffer from asthma all over the world. These children are receiving medication through machines called nebulizers in an asthma clinic in Uzbekistan.

an alarming pace, particularly in large cities such as New York City, Chicago, Boston, and San Diego.

The reason for the rising incidence of asthma in these areas is not entirely clear. If we knew the cause of the disease, we might be better able to explain these disturbing trends. Most scientists studying asthma today believe that the underlying problem is an increase in the number or activity of TH2 cells. But what causes this problem in TH2 cells, and why is it appearing so often?

Genetics definitely play a role in the development of asthma. The disease runs in families, even when members of a family are brought up separately in different environments.

Studies of identical twins have shown that if one twin has asthma, the other twin has a 60 to 70 percent chance of having asthma too.[3]

Some populations have a strikingly high incidence of asthma, an indication that they may carry a gene for asthma. Probably the highest incidence of asthma is on Tristan da Cunha, an extremely remote island in the middle of the South Atlantic Ocean, where 30 to 50 percent of the population has asthma.[4]

This island has an interesting history. It is a volcanic island, only 7 miles (11 km) in diameter. It was initially settled in 1816, when French emperor Napoléon Bonaparte was exiled to the island of St. Helena. The British were afraid Napoléon's supporters might use Tristan da Cunha as a base for a rescue attempt, so they stationed British troops there. One officer decided to stay behind when other troops left several years later. A few shipwreck survivors and some women from St. Helena joined the officer over the years. As a result, the population is probably descended from only about fifteen people. So the high incidence of asthma in this population may be due to a single gene that was inherited from one of the original settlers and passed down to all the descendants. Researchers are working to identify this gene.[5] A different group of scientists has already found another gene involved in the development of asthma.[6]

But even if all the "asthma genes" were identified, we would still not be able to predict exactly who would have asthma and who would not. The inheritance pattern of asthma is not simple. If your mother has asthma, or even if both your parents have asthma, you are not inevitably destined to develop asthma. Probably it takes multiple genes in combination with environmental factors to result in asthma.

Knowing which environmental factors are important and how they cause asthma is difficult. Why does one person develop asthma while another does not—even if both have the genetic predisposition? Several theories have been proposed. One theory holds that if the immune system is not exposed to infections early in life, it never develops the experience to fight infections properly. The T-cells do not learn how to respond to invaders. When individuals with inexperienced immune systems are later challenged by allergens they respond inappropriately with a TH2 response.

Another popular theory is that asthma is caused by exposure to certain irritants early in life when the immune system is still immature. If genetically susceptible people are exposed to a high dose of irritants early in life, the immune system may develop abnormally, with an exaggerated TH2 response—and the children may then develop asthma or other allergic diseases.

Both of these theories may help explain the recent epidemic of asthma. Outside the United States, most of the increase in asthma has taken place in developing areas—where improvements in hygiene and increased vaccination rates have dramatically decreased early childhood illness. The population is healthier overall, but people who were genetically prone to develop asthma now develop the disease. Their immune systems may not have had enough stimulation by infections.

In the United States and other industrialized countries, the greatest increases in asthma are among minority children in inner-city areas. These areas have very high rates of indoor and outdoor air pollution. They may be near expressways and factories where pollutants from cars and smokestacks poison the air. Smoking is common;

cockroaches, dust mites, and rodents thrive in areas of dense population and crowded living conditions. Poor ventilation and lack of air-conditioning also contribute to indoor pollution. Thus children in the inner cities are exposed to extremely high levels of irritants at a very early age. According to current theories, if they are genetically susceptible, they will develop asthma.

The possible link between air pollution and allergen exposure and the development of asthma has been borne out by several studies. A 1991 survey by the Centers for Disease Control and Prevention found that 63 percent of people with asthma lived in areas where pollution was highest.[7] And a 1994 study of children in New York City showed that up to 12 percent in some areas had asthma.[8] One school in New York City, Bronx Public School 48, was surrounded by sludge and waste plants. One-third of the students—and many of the teachers—had asthma. In contrast, Africans living in villages with limited transportation and no electricity, and eating a traditional diet, have very low rates of asthma.

The increasing incidence of asthma is probably due to a number of factors. Improved diagnosis, high pollution levels inside and outside the home, parental smoking, vaccinations, and other risk factors probably all play a role. Until we know exactly what causes the abnormal T-cell response, we cannot pinpoint the reason for the epidemic. In the meantime, we can work on controlling the factors that we know worsen the symptoms of the disease.

CHAPTER 4

The Course of Asthma

Asthma can develop at any stage of life, from early infancy to old age, but most people with asthma develop the disease early in life. About 40 percent of them develop symptoms before they are a year old. More than 80 percent develop asthma before age five.[1] Infants who wheeze do not always go on to develop asthma, however. Some grow out of their symptoms—as their airways get larger their symptoms disappear, never to return, while other wheezing infants go on to develop asthma. Adult-onset asthma is usually related to high levels of exposure to irritants in the workplace.

Most children with asthma have a definite allergic component—meaning they have specific triggers for their asthma. Usually wheezing and coughing episodes are infrequent and follow exposure to an allergen or a cold or other infection.

As they grow up, most children with asthma tend to get somewhat better. About 30 percent of children with asthma improve markedly and may be symptom-free by early adulthood. But remember that this does not mean they are free of the disease. Lung-function tests show that their airways are still not normal, and asthma symptoms may reappear later. Significant disease persists in approximately 60 percent of these people. Boys are more likely than girls to improve significantly as they grow older. The severity of asthma in childhood usually predicts the likelihood of continued disease. Children with severe persistent asthma will likely continue to suffer from the disease as they enter adulthood.

The course of asthma consists of acute attacks of varying severity. These asthma attacks can vary widely—from rare mild wheezing that may disappear for years at a time to frequent or even constant symptoms that may progress to very serious events. Episodes may gradually become more frequent and more severe. However, asthma is generally a chronic disease, not a progressive one. The lungs usually return to normal functioning if the inflammation is controlled.

Diagnosis

The symptoms of asthma vary greatly from one person to the next, so asthma is sometimes difficult to diagnose. Generally a person with asthma suffers from episodes of shortness of breath and wheezing. Symptoms are often worse at night. The person may even be able to give a history of attacks triggered by a particular stimulus, such as exercise, pollen, or stress. Some people, however, have only a cough that is especially troublesome at night. Others complain of tightness in the chest or fatigue when they exercise.

Diagnosing asthma requires a thorough history of symptoms and exposures, as well as a family history. Many other diseases mimic asthma. For example, heart disease can cause shortness of breath, chest tightness, and even wheezing. A foreign body in the airway—such as an inhaled piece of chicken bone or a peanut—can cause wheezing. Infections may cause chronic coughing.

A physical exam is necessary to check for other possible causes of the symptoms. The doctor may also look for problems commonly associated with asthma, such as sinusitis, runny nose, and skin rashes. Listening to the chest with a stethoscope, the doctor may hear the high-pitched wheezing sound of air moving through narrowed airways, even if the wheezing is not loud enough for the person with asthma to hear. Chest X rays can rule out an infection or foreign body as the cause of the wheezing and shortness of breath.

Often, however, the person with asthma has an entirely normal exam and chest X ray. The nature of the disease is that it waxes and wanes. And although we know that smoldering inflammation may be present inside the airways, it cannot be seen on a physical exam. Pulmonary-function tests may help in the diagnosis of asthma.

A pulmonary-function test measures the volume of air inside the lungs and how quickly air flows in and out of the lungs. The test shows if airflow is obstructed due to narrowing of the airways. If the airflow returns to normal after treatment with a drug to dilate the bronchi, then the person probably has asthma. These tests are done in a pulmonary-function laboratory, which has special equipment to measure the volume and flow of gases. In some tests, the person sits inside a box and closes the door. The box, called a plethysmograph, can measure the total amount of air inside the person's body—which includes the lungs. In other tests, the person breathes through a tube called a spirometer, which measures airflow.

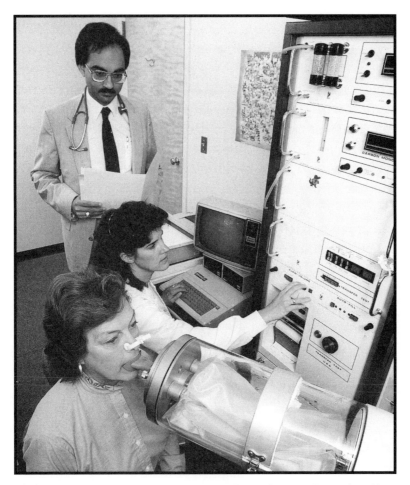

Pulmonary-function tests are conducted in a doctor's office or hospital.

The results of the pulmonary-function test are often normal in people with asthma. How can this be possible if the airways are inflamed and abnormal? The inflammation may narrow the airways somewhat, but not enough to decrease the flow of air. Unless the pulmonary-function test is done while a person is actually having an asthma attack, it may not show any abnormality.

A doctor who is not sure of a diagnosis of asthma may try to set off a mild asthma attack to see if the airways are hyperresponsive and become narrowed when stimulated. This test is also done in the pulmonary-function lab. Two common methods of provoking bronchoconstriction are exercise testing and the methacholine challenge. In an exercise test, people suspected of having asthma ride a bicycle or run on a treadmill while breathing cold air. Methacholine is a chemical irritant that, when inhaled, causes **bronchospasm** in some people. After exercising, or inhaling methacholine, the person repeats the pulmonary-function test. In people with asthma, the airways are hyper-responsive so, after this stimulus, their pulmonary-function test should show obstruction to airflow—indicating nar-rowing of the airways.

In very young children, pulmonary-function testing is not possible—so the doctor who suspects asthma may sim-ply begin treatment. If the symptoms improve, the child is tentatively diagnosed as having asthma. When the child is older, a pulmonary-function test can confirm the diagnosis.

After a diagnosis of asthma is made, monitoring is important. Periodic pulmonary-function tests can evaluate the course of the disease. With appropriate management, most people with asthma remain symptom-free. If people have recurrent symptoms, or if their pulmonary function deteriorates, their medical treatment should be reevaluated.

Types of Asthma

Asthma can range from a mild cough to recurrent life-threatening episodes of shortness of breath. This has led some people to think that what we call asthma may actually be several diseases all lumped under one name. Many attempts have been made to divide asthma into subtypes, based either on the cause of the disease or on its course. So far, none of these classification systems has caught on, and the groups often overlap. However, some of the common subtypes are described below.

Extrinsic, or Atopic, Versus Intrinsic Asthma

Extrinsic, or **atopic**, asthma is allergic asthma. *Extrinsic* means "from without" and *atopic* means "tending to have allergic reactions." Asthma attacks in these people are caused by something outside the body, such as pollen or animal hair. People with this type of asthma are often allergic to several substances and develop skin rashes and congestion as well as wheezing when exposed. This type of asthma usually starts during childhood, and the disease is often characterized by seasonal attacks when pollen counts are high.

Intrinsic asthma has less clear environmental triggers. *Intrinsic* means "from within," and people with this type of asthma do not usually have allergies to external substances. Onset is more often in adulthood. The problem with this classification system is that people thought to have intrinsic asthma often do have triggers, and the underlying airway abnormalities seem to be the same in both types of asthma. Today, this division between intrinsic and extrinsic asthma has fallen out of favor.

Exercise-Induced Asthma

Exercise-induced asthma is probably not a distinct type of asthma, since exercise causes bronchospasm in up to 90 percent of patients with asthma. Rapid breathing dehydrates the airways, causing irritation and triggering bronchoconstriction. Symptoms usually start several minutes after starting physical activity and peak about ten minutes after stopping exercise. The symptoms tend to fade about thirty minutes later. People who have symptoms only when they are physically active have pure exercise-induced asthma—but whether this is a distinct disease or merely a mild form of asthma is not clear.

Occupational Asthma

Occupational asthma is asthma triggered by exposure in the workplace. It usually begins in adulthood and is related to exposure to high levels of irritants, including disinfectants in hospitals, fumes in welding plants, and flour in bakeries. This category makes up about 2 percent of all asthmatics and occurs in a variety of occupations. For example, nurses and doctors can have asthmatic reactions to their latex surgical gloves.

Aspirin-Induced Asthma

Some people with asthma have severe reactions to aspirin and other pain medications. Usually these people have had asthma for years before developing a sensitivity to aspirin. Often they also have nasal polyps (growths in the nose), sinusitis, and rhinorrhea (runny nose).

Cough-Variant Asthma

In cough-variant asthma, the only symptom is a frequent or chronic cough that is not related to a cold or other infection. The sleep of people with this condition is often disturbed by coughing. The diagnosis can be made with pulmonary-function tests or peak flow meter readings when the person is symptomatic. (A peak flow meter is a portable device used to measure airflow.) Cough-variant asthma may also be merely a mild form of asthma.

Nocturnal Asthma

Asthma is often worse at night. Normal daily changes in hormone levels may cause this variation in symptoms. Allergens in the bedroom—such as dust mites in the bedding—may also play a role. Some people have symptoms only at night, and they are sometimes labeled as having nocturnal asthma. However, nocturnal asthma is more likely just poorly controlled asthma.

Brittle Asthma

Some people have what is termed brittle asthma. Their pulmonary function varies widely, and they can have sudden attacks of severe wheezing and shortness of breath. Management can be difficult, since there is often little warning before an attack. They may have normal airflow one minute, and only 50 percent of normal flow rates the next. People with brittle asthma are at higher risk for serious complications than other people with asthma, but with careful management and the regular use of preventive medications, their disease can be controlled.

The Costs of Asthma

Asthma often has emotional and physical effects on a person's life. We can keep records of hospitalization rates, number of days of school or work missed, and the costs of care. But the most important effects are probably emotional. Asthma is a lifelong chronic condition that requires daily attention. This puts stress on people with asthma, as well as on their family and friends. It is hard to estimate these kinds of costs, so we often focus on the physical and financial effects on people's lives and on society.

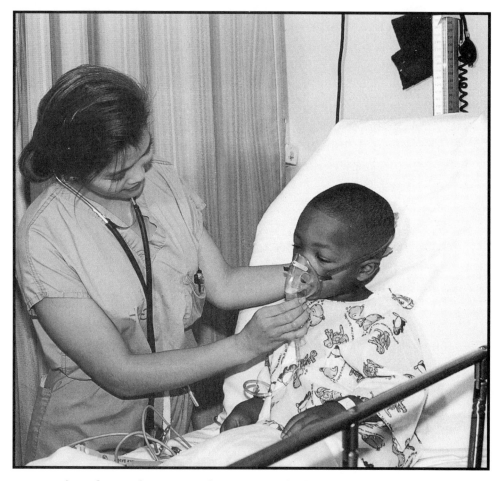

Attacks send many asthmatics to the hospital. This young patient receives medication through a nebulizer.

In most cases, asthma causes no long-term damage to the airways. If the underlying inflammation can be controlled, lung function returns to normal. However, some studies have shown that normal lung growth may be impaired in children with severe and persistent symptoms. In adults, the presence of asthma in combination with other lung diseases results in decreased lung function.

The increase in asthma cases in the last fifteen years has been accompanied by an increase in hospital admissions. Here too, the greatest increases are in the inner cities of the United States. A 1999 analysis of hospitalization rates in New York City showed that the areas of the city with the lowest average income had the highest rates of hospitalization—even when adjusted for the increased incidence of asthma in these areas.[2] So people with asthma in lower socioeconomic groups are hospitalized more often than are asthma sufferers with higher incomes. The reason for this could be that the people of lower socioeconomic status have more severe asthma, so they end up in the hospital more often. Or it may be that, although their asthma is no more severe, people with lower income have more trouble controlling it. It is a probably a combination of these factors.

People who live in poorer urban areas have increased exposure to indoor and outdoor pollution due to poor housing conditions and frequent proximity to factories, dumps, or highways. And often they have little or no access to preventive medical care. Most do not have a regular doctor and receive medical care only in the emergency room. They obviously do not get the education and preventive medications needed to control asthma and prevent attacks.

Although deaths from asthma are rare, they occur in 1 to 2 percent of people with severe asthma. Each year, more than 4,000 people die of asthma in the United States, and 40,000 die worldwide. **Mortality** rates have increased dramatically since 1980, despite our new understanding of the disease and more effective treatments. Mortality increased 52 percent for African-Americans and 45 percent for Caucasians from 1980 to 1990. Again, the areas with the highest death rates are the poorest inner-city neighborhoods.[3]

Despite new treatments and new understanding of the disease, asthma continues to cause serious illness, disability, and even death, especially among the poorest segments of our society. On the plus side, we have seen that the rates of hospitalization and death fall significantly in populations that receive education and preventive care.

The people most likely to become increasingly ill are those with the following risk factors: frequent severe attacks, failure to take medications correctly, poor access to health care, serious family problems, African-American and other minority groups, age in the late teens, and inner-city residence. All these risk factors would seem to be related to a lack of preventive care. With proper medical care and education about the disease, most people with asthma can have full, healthy lives.

How to Prevent Asthma Attacks

We often read of sports stars, rock singers, performers, or politicians who have asthma. With the help of doctors and other health professionals, they have learned to manage their disease. The goal of asthma management is to allow the person with asthma to live a normal, active life with slight or no symptoms and few treatment side effects. As you now know, asthma is a disease that has been recognized for several thousand years, and people have been looking for effective treatments or cures all that time. Some of the ancient treatments are not that different from current recommendations.

Now we know that asthma is a chronic, lifelong condition that is always present, though it may change in severity and may go into long periods of remission when no symptoms are present. Today we direct treatment at the underlying disorder that leads to the attacks. And with our new understanding of immune-system mechanisms, we see that the disease may someday be cured.

Asthma is caused by an interaction between the immune system and the linings of the airways. It creates

51

hyperresponsive airways that are likely to become narrowed when exposed to triggers. Treatment is aimed at not only controlling the asthma symptoms, but also at reducing or eliminating the inflammation of the airways. With less inflammation, we prevent damage to the airways and break the cycle of repeated irritation, inflammation, and bronchoconstriction.

The first step in treating asthma is to identify triggers and find ways to avoid them. Triggers are situations or substances that lead to an asthma attack. They set off the cascade of events that lead to inflammation and bronchoconstriction. Avoiding these triggers can prevent the vicious cycle of inflammation and bronchoconstriction. Also, some people think that exposure to these triggers in childhood may contribute to the development of asthma in susceptible individuals. They believe that if the inflammatory response can be avoided, the airways will not become hyperresponsive, and asthma may not develop.

Identifying Triggers

Possible triggers are all around us—animals, dust mites, molds, grasses, trees, pollens, cockroaches, pollutants, tobacco smoke, cold air, and exercise. It seems impossible to avoid all these things. We would probably have to live in a sterile plastic bubble. However, each person has specific triggers that are especially potent, and we need to find out what those specific triggers are. Also, decreasing exposure to any airway irritant can be helpful.

Asthma Diaries

A good first step in managing asthma is to keep an asthma diary—a daily record of all the factors that affect your asthma. You need to write down symptoms, daily activities and exposures, peak flow readings—home measurements of lung function—and medications. You can also use the diary to record your emotions—fear, anger, frustration, or happiness—because emotional factors can play a role in triggering an asthma attack. Since most triggers cause both an immediate and a delayed inflammatory response, it is not always easy to interpret the diary. However, when reviewed with a doctor, it can help you figure out which exposures may be triggering the attacks.

Asthma sufferers often keep a daily record, or diary, of their peak flow readings.

Skin Testing

Skin testing is a procedure that can help people whose asthma has an allergic or atopic component. In skin testing, doctors expose the skin to allergens—substances that cause allergies—and then look for a local inflammatory response, such as redness, swelling, or itching, in the skin around the exposure. The allergen is usually injected just under the skin with a small needle or scratched on the surface of the skin. The procedure is painless and usually bloodless. If the skin shows a reaction, the substance may be a trigger. Skin testing is not done often and should be done only under a doctor's supervision, since even this small exposure can sometimes lead to a severe response that might require medication.

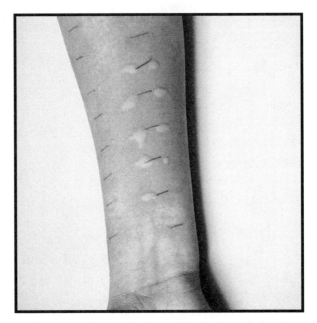

A patient's arm after receiving skin-testing injections shows reactions to several allergens.

Common Triggers and How to Create a Trigger-Free World

Once you learn which triggers seem to cause your attacks, you can begin trying to avoid them. Here are some of the most common triggers and trigger-management techniques.

Smoking

Smoking is the worst asthma trigger. Almost everyone with asthma reacts to cigarette smoke. Smoking tobacco, marijuana, cocaine, or any other substance delivers an extremely concentrated level of pollution directly into the lungs. Even one cigarette can trigger an asthmatic attack. And, in addition to triggering acute bronchospasm, smoking causes severe inflammation in the lungs. Tobacco smoke also affects the functioning of the important mucocilliary escalator—so the lungs' ability to get rid of foreign particles is harmed by smoking. The lungs become more susceptible to infection and less able to clear out other irritants. All these factors make the lungs even more hyperresponsive, and this hyperresponsiveness can last for weeks after smoking only one cigarette, cigar, or pipe.

Second-hand or passive smoking—exposure to another person's cigarette smoke—may also cause bronchospasm. Children of smokers seem to have a higher incidence and severity of asthma. Neither the person with asthma nor any family members should smoke, and smoke-filled bars or parties should be avoided. Tobacco smoke also contributes to heart disease, cancer, emphysema, and other diseases. So the family might want to thank their members with asthma for helping them quit smoking.

Air Pollution—Indoors and Outdoors

Environmental pollution—high levels of particles and industrial by-products in the air—also irritates the lungs. The increase of asthma in urban centers may be due in part to air pollution, although this has been difficult to prove. Surprisingly, studies have shown that asthma rates are actually lower in eastern European countries where the air quality is worse. Also, it is not clear whether more asthma attacks occur on days with higher pollution levels, and more study needs to be done on this. Several epidemics of asthma have been related to air pollution—for example, in Barcelona, Spain, and in New Orleans, Louisiana. In these two cities, the epidemics were apparently due to soybean dust in the air from soybean shipments unloaded on the docks.

It is not always possible to live in areas with clean air. We cannot always choose where we live just by the quality of the air. Perhaps new efforts at controlling air pollution will improve the situation for people with asthma. Air-conditioning can help filter out some of the pollution inside the home.

In some occupations, workers are exposed to inhaled irritants. People with asthma who find that their symptoms are worse at work may be reacting to an irritant in their workplace. Federal law requires employers to try to accommodate people with occupational asthma. Mask filters, though uncomfortable, may decrease exposure. Medication taken before work may control symptoms. In severe cases, however, people with work-related asthma may need to change their occupations.

Wood smoke from fireplaces and wood-burning stoves may also cause problems for people with asthma. To avoid this trigger, they need to use gas, oil, or electric heat. Cleaning fluids, perfumes, air fresheners, hair sprays, lotions, and other scented substances are another form of air pollution and may trigger asthma attacks. If these substances are a problem, people with asthma and all their close contacts should try to avoid using perfumed products.

Dust Mites and Cockroaches

The dust mite lives in the dust found in most homes. It is a microscopic creature with eight legs—an arachnid—that feeds on the flakes of skin shed by humans and lives in mattresses and other soft furnishings. Dust mites have been recognized as asthma triggers since the 1960s, but even as long ago as the 1700s it was noted that people who handled old mattresses and dusty old clothes were prone to asthma attacks. Cockroaches have thrived throughout history and live in many human dwellings, feeding on scraps of decaying food. The feces of both dust mites and cockroaches dry up and float into the air, where these particles are inhaled and may trigger asthmatic attacks in sensitive individuals. Most children with asthma are sensitive to both household dust mites and cockroaches.[1]

If possible, a person with asthma should live in a well-ventilated home. Frequent vacuuming and washing bed linens, pillows, and stuffed animals weekly in very hot water can reduce the numbers of dust mites and cockroach feces. Vacuuming stirs up dust and allergens though, so the sensitive person should stay away while it is being done. If that is not possible, a dust mask can help. It takes at least half an hour for the dust to settle again. Removing carpeting, curtains, and upholstered furniture, especially from the bedroom, and using special pillow and mattress covers can also decrease the allergens in the home. Dust mites like a warm, moist environment, so air conditioners and dehumidifiers may help to decrease the infestation. Avoid attracting cockroaches by keeping all food in covered containers—and never eat in the bedroom. Pesticides can get rid of cockroaches but are rarely effective against dust mites.

A dust mite, seen here through a microscope, feeds on shedded skin. Its feces are thought to trigger allergic reactions to dust.

Furred and Feathered Creatures

Sensitivity to animals and birds is extremely common among people with asthma, especially those with atopic asthma. Some people may be sensitive to several kinds of animals, others may be allergic to just one. Cats are the most common cause of allergic responses, but there is no such thing as an allergen-free animal—dogs, horses, birds, rats, mice, and virtually any other creature can cause attacks. The offending agent—the trigger—may be dander. Dander consists of particles of hair, skin, feathers, saliva, urine, or feces that can float in the air or may be left behind on a cat or dog's favorite chair.

People who are allergic to one animal usually develop sensitivities to other animals if they have repeated contact. Therefore doctors recommend that people with asthma who are sensitive to animals not live with any pets. This recommendation is not always easy to follow, however. It is often hard to give up a beloved pet. And in inner cities, for example, where rats are a problem, people may have to choose between cats or rodents. One woman in New York City with a child with asthma and a pet cat stated her case in the *New York Times.* "Where I live you can't go to the store without seeing a rat. If that cat will stop me from having [rats], then I'm willing to sit all night with Kevin in the hospital if I have to."[2] It is hard, too, to give up a large dog that provides protection in a rough neighborhood. If pets must be kept in the house, they should be banned from the bedrooms. It may be helpful to wash the animals (including cats) weekly to remove dried saliva from their fur, thus reducing the allergens. Running a damp mop over the walls, floors, and ceiling weekly can also decrease the amount of dander in the air.

Plants and Fungi

Various plants and fungi release substances into the air that can provoke an allergic response in susceptible people. The pollen from grasses, trees, and weeds consists of small airborne particles that can be inhaled. Usually, the pollen particles are too large to enter into the lower airways and cause only a runny nose (rhinitis), or itchy eyes (conjunctivitis). However, they sometimes break up into smaller particles, which can be inhaled into the bronchi and provoke an asthma attack. "Hay fever" is the term used when the trigger is ragweed pollen.

Different plants release pollen at different times of year. People who are sensitive to a specific pollen may have symptoms that change during the year, in accordance with the levels of that specific pollen. For example, many trees release their pollen in the fall, so a person with sensitivity to tree pollen may have more frequent or severe asthma attacks every fall. Vegetation varies throughout the world, and the timing of pollen release—even for the same plants—may also vary. Some fungal spores are released on a seasonal basis, other molds thrive in damp areas, and in the right conditions, such as a damp building or cellar, may cause symptoms year-round.

It is a good idea to find out whether pollens or molds trigger a person's asthma—either by an asthma diary or skin testing. Controlling the moisture in the home with air conditioners or dehumidifiers, keeping windows closed during the pollen season, and fixing leaky faucets can help. Humidifiers, on the other hand, are a bad idea. Pollen and spore counts are highest in the middle of the day and afternoon, so people with asthma can sometimes avoid attacks by planning their outdoor activities for early in the morning. The doctor may be able to adjust therapy to seasons of the year when pollen concentrations in the air are high. Pollen filters are available, but they are often expensive or inconvenient.

Food and Drink

Some triggers are not inhaled but swallowed. Food products rarely trigger asthma, but a particular dye or preservative can occasionally cause an asthma attack. Sulfites—chemicals used as food preservatives—are probably the most common culprit in this category. They are found in dried fruits, shrimp, processed potatoes, beer, and wine. Every once in a while, you hear of a person who dies of an allergic reaction after eating a certain food, such as peanuts. This is a very rare type of severe allergy called **anaphylaxis**. An anaphylactic reaction is a sudden, massive inflammatory response, with severe bronchoconstriction, and it must be treated immediately. Although people with anaphylactic reactions have bronchoconstriction and wheezing, they do not necessarily have asthma. Their reaction is an isolated problem and is not associated with the chronic or recurrent symptoms of asthma.

The best way to find out if a food, drink, or medication is making your asthma worse is to keep an asthma diary, listing all meals and snacks in detail. Skin testing is rarely helpful in identifying food allergies. Once the offending triggers have been identified, they should be avoided. That means reading lists of ingredients on food packages and checking with the cook at home or the staff at a restaurant. This can be difficult, since all the preservatives or dyes in a food may not be listed in the ingredients, and restaurants may include some surprising ingredients in certain dishes. Peanuts may be used in making chili, for example, or shrimp paste may be included in a vegetarian dumpling. Anyone who has a severe food allergy or has had an anaphylactic reaction in the past may need to carry a special medication at all times to treat an allergic reaction on the spot.

Drugs and Alcohol

Aspirin, ibuprofen, and other pain medications trigger severe asthma attacks in some people, but acetaminophen (Tylenol) is usually safe. In general, people with asthma should check with their doctor before taking any over-the-counter medication. Medications prescribed by a doctor for other conditions may also cause bronchospasm. Some people have anaphylactic reactions to medications—especially to antibiotics such as penicillin. Whenever you are seeing a doctor, even for an unrelated problem such as a broken arm, you should tell the doctor that you have asthma.

Alcohol, cocaine, marijuana, heroin, and other drugs also pose special dangers for people with asthma. Inhaled drugs such as crack cocaine and marijuana or intranasally applied drugs should never be used by a person with asthma. These drugs are directly irritating to the airways and can trigger attacks. They also cause long-term damage to the lungs, which people with asthma cannot afford. Other drugs that are not inhaled are also dangerous for people with asthma. Drugs that alter the state of consciousness may make the person with asthma less likely to take the actions needed to control an attack and may decrease their basic drive to breathe. An asthma attack in a person high on drugs or alcohol can be very dangerous. Chronic use of drugs or alcohol may also lead to poor compliance with treatment, leading to poor control of asthma and more frequent and severe attacks.

Exercise and Climate

Climate and exercise can trigger asthma in some people, but these triggers cannot be avoided. In most people with asthma, cold air triggers bronchospasm, perhaps because inhaling cold air leads to heat loss and damage to the airway linings. Thunderstorms and high winds have also been said to worsen asthma—perhaps because the pressure changes and winds break up the pollen and spores into fragments small enough to be inhaled into the lower airways.

Taking medication before exercise helps people who suffer from exercise-induced asthma prevent attacks.

Exercise-induced asthma is particularly common among children and young people with asthma. In some studies, exercise was shown to cause bronchospasm in up to 90 percent of people with asthma. The mechanism is unclear, but is probably related to the rapid breathing that produces heat loss and dehydration and thus damages the airway lining. Even slight exertion may produce breathlessness, despite overall good conditioning. Fear of an asthmatic attack often leads people to limit their participation in sports. However, although physical exertion may trigger an asthma attack, exercise and good cardiopulmonary conditioning reduce bronchial hyperresponsiveness and improve pulmonary functioning in the long run.

So how can a person with exercise-induced asthma manage to exercise and participate in sports? Using medications prior to the exposure may prevent the inflammatory response. The new long-acting bronchodilators are particularly effective for this purpose. Exercising outdoors on a cold day is more likely to trigger an attack, but wearing a scarf over the mouth in winter may decrease symptoms. Doctors may need to give additional medications in the winter months.

Swimming indoors in a warm pool seems to be one of the activities least likely to provoke asthma, perhaps because the warm humid air prevents dehydration and heat loss in the lower airways. Therefore swimming may be a good conditioning exercise for patients with severe exercise-induced asthma, or with extreme fear of attacks. Once they are more confident of their abilities and have improved cardiopulmonary conditioning, they can expand into other sports activities. A warm-up period of stretching and low-level exercises before exertion can also help decrease symptoms. However, while this may be practical before gym class or a soccer game, it is not possible to spend five minutes warming up before running to catch the school bus.

Medical Conditions

Illness can also cause asthma attacks. Infections of the respiratory tract produce symptoms similar to an allergic response—cough, runny nose, and sneezing. In addition, airway reactivity increases during and after a viral infection—probably because of inflammation of the membranes. People with asthma may benefit from a yearly vaccine against influenza virus. Increasing medication doses in the flu season or during and after a viral infection may also help control or prevent asthma attacks.

Sinus infections and nasal polyps may also worsen asthma. Chronic headaches, low-grade fever, or nasal congestion are signs that one of these conditions is present. Treating the sinusitis may be helpful. Removing nasal polyps also helps some people with asthma control their symptoms.

Other conditions too can worsen asthma. In a condition called a gastroesophageal reflux, acid from the stomach backs up into the esophagus, and sometimes all the way up into the back of the throat where it can then flow down into the airways. Gastric acid is extremely irritating to the airways, causing inflammation, which may lead to an asthma attack. Thyroid disease can also affect asthma. Overproduction of thyroid hormone worsens asthma, while underproduction decreases the responsiveness of the airways.

A person who has been managing asthma well, but whose condition has become more troublesome, should tell a doctor. Another treatable disorder may be making the asthma more severe.

Emotions and Hormones

Normal changes in the body's condition can also lead to asthma attacks. Emotional excitement in some people may trigger bronchospasm. Laughing or crying may sometimes cause rapid breathing, or hyperventilation, and result in the same symptoms as exercise-induced bronchospasm. Stress causes changes in the nervous system and various chemicals are released that can trigger bronchospasm in people with hyperreactive airways. We also know that the nervous system and the immune system are linked, and long-term stress affects the immune system, making people more likely to develop infections that may then trigger their asthma.[3]

Other emotional states may also interfere with asthma management. For example, a depressed or anxious person may have trouble taking medication regularly. People often find it hard to accept the diagnosis of a chronic condition. They may deny it and neglect the necessary management measures. It is important to follow instructions and take medication regularly—even when emotionally upset. With the appropriate medication and avoidance of triggers, asthma can be well controlled and people with asthma can live a normal, active life.

The various stages of growing up and their hormonal changes can also affect the course of asthma. Childhood asthma is more common in boys, and adult asthma is more common in women. Many women also describe changes in their asthma symptoms over the course of their menstrual cycle. During pregnancy, asthma may become either easier or more difficult to control. These observations show that hormonal levels may play a role in the severity of bronchospasm. This is not surprising, since we know that hormones help regulate the immune system, which plays a major role in asthma.

An asthma diary can help you find out if emotional or hormonal factors play a role in the course of your asthma. Some people like to use their asthma diary to write down their thoughts, wishes, or feelings of frustration or anger. Sometimes writing down feelings helps a person to understand and deal with them. A recent scientific study has shown that spending some time writing about a difficult or traumatic experience actually reduces asthma symptoms.[4] Showing these parts of the diary to a doctor, a trusted friend, or a counselor may help the person with asthma to understand their feelings better and find ways to cope with them.

After reviewing the diary, the doctor can adjust the medication regimen—perhaps giving additional or different medication before each menstrual cycle or before bedtime. Relaxation techniques, such as taking walks, listening to music, or counseling may help if emotional factors seem to be playing a role in asthma attacks.

CHAPTER 6

Treatment of Asthma

It is impossible to arrange one's life to avoid all triggers. Everyday life—going to school or to work, taking a train, riding on an elevator, or going to the movies—brings us in contact with thousands of possible triggers. The best anyone can do is avoid as many known triggers as possible. After that, a person with asthma needs an appropriate medical regimen—a regular schedule of medications prescribed specifically for that individual. The number of drugs and devices available for the treatment of asthma is enormous and increases every year. A medical regimen needs to be planned, with attention to the individual's age, the severity and frequency of symptoms, the type of asthma, and the person's ability and motivation to follow specific treatment regimens. The best treatment for anyone with asthma must be determined with a doctor.

How the Medications Are Taken

A doctor can prescribe pills or liquids to take by mouth, sprays for the nose or mouth, or injections under the skin or directly into the bloodstream.

Medications taken by mouth are the easiest to take and their effect is the longest. However, they can have more side effects, higher doses may be needed to achieve the same effect in the lungs, and they don't work immediately. They are first broken down in the stomach and then absorbed into the bloodstream.

Injected medications, either subcutaneous (under the skin) or intravenous (into the vein), are used mainly in the emergency room or hospital when someone has an acute, severe asthma attack. High doses of potent medications can be given this way. Drugs injected into the bloodstream work almost immediately.

Inhaled medications are now the most popular types for asthma. When a drug is inhaled through the mouth, some of the medication goes directly to the lungs where it has a local effect and is also absorbed through the membranes into the bloodstream. The rest of the medication is swallowed and absorbed through the gastrointestinal tract like an oral medication. Inhaled therapy provides high doses of medication directly to the airways and usually works very quickly. Much lower levels of drug enter the system, so inhaled medications tend to have fewer side effects than oral or injected drugs.

However, the delivery devices are often difficult to use properly and about half the people who use inhalers probably do not use them correctly. An effective inhaler device must provide a dose of medication made up of particles small enough and delivered at a high enough velocity to reach the lower airways. Two common inhaler devices are metered-dose inhalers (MDIs) and dry powder inhalers (DPIs).

Most asthma drugs are available in MDIs. These are small handheld devices that contain pressurized medication in a canister. Pressing down on the canister releases a measured dose of the drug. But using an MDI can be difficult. The user shakes the canister and breathes out before each dose, then inhales fully while activating the MDI and holds the breath for ten seconds. If the MDI is not activated at the beginning of inhalation, or if the breath is cut short, the drug will end up on the inside of the mouth—not in the lungs where it can do some good. This coordinated action is sometimes difficult. The doctor or nurse should demonstrate the correct method and watch the patient practice to

A tennis player uses a metered-dose inhaler (MDI) with an attachment called a spacer.

be sure it is done correctly. It is easy to fall into bad habits—so the patient should repeat this practice at every doctor's visit.

A spacer is an attachment that can be added to an MDI to make it easier to use. One end of the spacer is attached to the MDI and the drug is inhaled through the other end. With a spacer, the user simply has to activate the MDI and then breathe normally to inhale the drug particles floating in the spacer chamber. When a spacer is used, more medicine reaches the lower airways and less is left on the tongue or in the back of the throat.

DPIs (dry powder inhalers) are also handheld devices that deliver a measured dose of medication. When the person breathes in, the inhaler is activated. These devices may be difficult for young children, or for anyone in the grip of a severe asthma attack, because a certain amount of force is needed to activate them. Some of the common types of DPIs are spinhalers, turbohalers, and diskhalers.

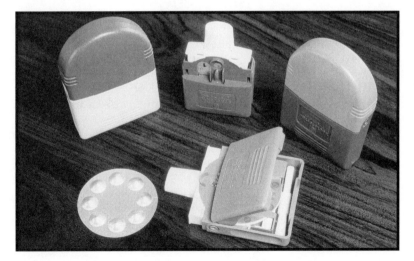

Diskhalers, activated by inhalation, deliver drugs in powder form directly to the lungs to treat asthma.

Most MDIs today use substances called chlorofluoro-carbons (CFCs) to propel the aerosol (the substance dispensed from a pressurized canister). When scientists discovered that CFCs damage the earth's ozone layer, an international ban was imposed on CFCs. However, MDIs have been exempted from this ban, until effective non-CFC inhalers can be developed. DPIs do not use CFCs, and other types of non-CFC inhalers are being developed.

Nebulizers are machines that use a flow of air or oxygen to provide a continuous dose of medication as an aerosol through the nose or through a mouthpiece. These machines are about the size of a shoebox, but they provide high doses of the drug quickly and are useful for infants or young children and in acute asthma attacks. Nebulizers are often used in emergency rooms and hospitals for the treatment of acute asthma attacks.

The Drugs

At least six different kinds of drugs are now in common use. There are also several other new or experimental drugs. Some medications are given daily to prevent attacks, others are used before exposure to a known trigger, and still others are used to relieve the symptoms of an attack. We can divide medications into two main types. Preventive drugs reduce inflammation and hyperresponsiveness, while symptomatic drugs relieve symptoms.

Anti-Inflammatory/Preventive Drugs

We now understand that the wheezing and shortness of breath that make up an asthma attack are caused by inflammation. Therefore, doctors now try to treat or prevent the inflammation and thus prevent asthma attacks from starting. The three main types of anti-inflammatory drugs are **steroids**, **cromones**, and **anti-leukotrienes**.

Steroids

Steroids are drugs that mimic normal body hormones called corticosteroids and reduce inflammation throughout the body. Corticosteroids are hormones produced by the adrenal glands, which are located above the kidneys. In the body, these hormones have multiple functions—including control of carbohydrate, fat, and protein metabolism and immune-system regulation. Synthetic corticosteroids were developed in the 1950s and are used in the treatment of many diseases, including asthma. Steroids can pass directly into all the cells in the body and affect their actions.

In regard to immune-system regulation, steroids make the cells increase their production of anti-inflammatory agents and decrease their production of inflammatory agents. They also may make the cell resistant to the effects of chemicals from other cells, and they probably increase the production and sensitivity of beta-receptors. These effects occur in any cell of the body that the steroid enters. The result in the airways is dramatically decreased inflammation and hyperresponsiveness, as well as improved response to another class of asthma medication, the **beta-agonists** (see below).

This powerful anti-inflammatory action is very effective in the treatment of asthma. When steroids interrupt the inflammatory cascade, the vicious cycle of recurrent or persistent bronchospasm is broken. However, the steroids have two disadvantages. Steroids take about six hours to act and they do not relieve bronchospasm that is already present. Also, as would be expected of a drug that can affect every cell in the body, steroids may have many side effects.

73

The anti-inflammatory action of steroids also affects the normal functioning of the immune system, so people taking high-dose steroids for a long period of time may be more susceptible to infections. Adrenal insufficiency may also develop after prolonged use because taking synthetic corticosteroids fools the body into believing that it has adequate amounts of all types of steroids, so the normal production of steroid hormones is suppressed. In times of stress, such as illness, the increased production of steroid hormones helps the body increase its metabolism to provide energy and support the blood pressure. People who have been taking steroids for a prolonged period may be unable to produce the large amount of steroids necessary in a stressful situation because their glands are out of practice. If the body cannot respond to stress, even a minor illness can become serious, and a serious illness can become life-threatening unless extra doses of corticosteroids are given.

Long-term steroid use may cause other side effects. Metabolic changes include brittle bones (osteoporosis), excess body fluid accumulation (edema), thin, easily bruised skin, abnormal fat deposition, cataracts, high blood pressure, diabetes, muscle breakdown, acne, changes in body-hair distribution, and growth impairment in children. Psychiatric changes may also occur—including mood swings, elation or depression, and sometimes even delusions.

These side effects sound scary, but remember that they do not occur in everyone, many are rare, and most are unlikely at the doses used for the treatment of asthma. With higher doses and prolonged treatment over many years, the risks of developing side effects increases. A few people with severe asthma need repeated or prolonged courses of oral steroids. Doctors are searching for ways to use steroids that will minimize the side effects, while still controlling the diseases they are used to treat.

Steroids can be taken by mouth, injected into the veins, or inhaled. In a severe asthma attack, doctors inject high doses of steroids into the veins with intravenous catheters. This route of administration is extremely potent and is used to control the inflammation and break the cycle of repeated bronchoconstriction in people admitted to the hospital with severe asthma attacks.

Oral steroids are extremely effective in controlling asthma and are easy to take. However, long-term use risks the side effects described earlier. For this reason, doctors try to avoid prolonged use of oral steroids, especially in young people. Short courses—up to three weeks—are used to control an acute asthma attack, with few minor side effects and virtually no serious ones. It is important to follow the doctor's directions carefully in taking steroids, since abruptly stopping the drug can lead to recurrence of wheezing or, rarely, to adrenal insufficiency. Someone who has been taking oral or intravenous steroids for a significant length of time may need to reduce the dose very slowly over several days to several weeks or even months.

The development of inhaled steroids in the 1950s was a breakthrough in the treatment of asthma. Inhaled steroids provide the desired anti-inflammatory benefits in the lungs, with virtually no side effects in the rest of the body. Inhaled steroids are therefore the most important preventive agents for patients with moderate and severe asthma. The drug must be used daily to prevent asthma attacks, may take several weeks to have full effect, and is not useful in reversing acute bronchospasm. An example of an inhaled steroid is fluticasone (trade name, Flovent).

Side effects with the newer inhaled steroids at regular doses are slight. However, at very high doses or in small children, some studies indicate there may be systemic effects. It is important to rinse the mouth after using inhaled steroids to prevent dysphonia—a change in voice—and avoid suppression of the local immune system, which would allow the development of oral "thrush," a fungal growth in the mouth.

Nasal steroids are sometimes given to patients with allergic rhinitis, or runny nose. If the rhinitis is controlled, there seems to be an improvement in the asthma too. Nasal steroids have to be used regularly.

Cromones

The group of drugs called cromones are now a popular treatment for children and for some adults with moderate asthma. It is not clear exactly how these drugs work in the body, but in laboratory studies, they seem to make some cells, particularly mast cells, less leaky and prevent them from causing inflammation. Cromones may also inhibit sensory-nerve fibers and make them less unstable or hyper-responsive. Thus, cromones may reduce the inflammation and hyperresponsiveness of asthma.

Cromones are usually inhaled, and they may be used in a nebulizer. People with food sensitivities that trigger their asthma may occasionally use an oral version. After long-term use—several weeks at least—cromones reduce airway hyperresponsiveness and can prevent attacks from starting, thus helping to control asthma. They can also be used before exposure to a known trigger, especially exercise, to reduce the likelihood of bronchospasm. Cromones do not help an acute asthma attack once it begins, however. A major advantage of these drugs is that they have virtually no side effects.

Anti-Leukotriene Agents

An exciting new development in asthma treatment is the discovery of ways to block the action of leukotrienes. Leukotrienes are substances released by leukocytes, or white blood cells. Certain leukotrienes play an important role in inflammation and in the asthma cascade, causing bronchospasm, edema, and chemotaxis. Scientists have developed agents that either decrease the production of leukotrienes or inhibit their action.

In 1996, the first of these agents became available for medical use in the United States. Early studies indicate that these agents, in oral or inhaled form, are effective for some kinds of asthma. The studies included people with asthma caused by cold, exercise, and aspirin, as well as allergies. The drugs seem to have few side effects—mainly headache, stomach upset and, rarely, some liver toxicity. An example is montelukast (trade name, Singulair). Further studies of long-term use have yet to be completed. These agents have enormous potential since leukotrienes affect many parts of the body.

Immunosuppressants

Many other drugs suppress the immune system and can thus decrease the inflammation of asthma. Some have been tried on people with severe asthma in an effort re- duce their steroid use. However, most immunosuppres- sants have their own side effects and do not work any better than steroids, so they are not a good choice for asthma treatment.

Bronchodilator/Symptomatic Drugs

Since there is no cure for asthma yet, and none of the preventive drugs are 100 percent effective, we still need treatments for the symptoms of acute asthma attacks.

Beta Adrenergic Receptor Agonists

The first-line agents for the treatment of acute asthma attacks are called the beta adrenergic receptor agonists, or beta-agonists. Many of the drugs used today are designed to make the body's mechanisms work better—or to stop the body's mechanisms from doing something that causes problems. Beta-agonists act by binding receptors in cell walls called beta-receptors. Every cell in the body has many types of receptors embedded in its walls. Various substances, circulating in the blood or released by nearby cells, come in contact with these receptors and bind to them if the substances are the right fit. It works like two pieces of a puzzle locking together. When these pieces come together, they trigger a chain of events inside the cell. Many drugs work by binding cellular receptors and either activating the receptor or blocking the binding site so that it cannot become activated. Agonists are substances that activate the receptor while antagonists or blockers prevent the normal activation of the receptor.

The beta-receptors are one type of receptor. When these receptors are activated in the lungs, they cause relaxation of the smooth muscles surrounding the airways (leading to bronchodilation), improved clearance of mucus by the cilia, and other effects. Beta-agonist drugs activate these beta-receptors and thus relieve the bronchoconstriction of an acute asthma attack and may also improve mucus clearance. Beta-agonists can be taken orally, inhaled, or injected under the skin.

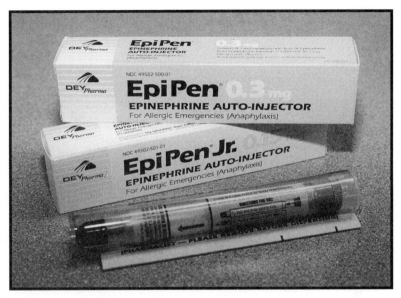

Epi-pens are used in allergic emergencies.

Epinephrine, a natural hormone made in the adrenal gland, acts as a beta-agonist. It was identified in the early twentieth century and has been used for the treatment of acute asthma attacks ever since. And we have also discovered that the plant *ma huang,* used by the Chinese since ancient times, contains a substance similar to epinephrine.

Injections of epinephrine activate the beta-receptors and are used for acute severe attacks in the emergency room or in the doctor's office. Unfortunately, the effects of epinephrine last only a short time, so it must be combined with other treatments. Epinephrine injections are also used to treat anaphylaxis—an acute severe allergic response. People with a history of severe allergies or anaphylaxis can carry small devices called "epi-pens" to give themselves an injection of epinephrine in an emergency. Epinephrine has side effects, including a racing heart, nervousness, and high blood pressure.

Several beta-agonists work only on a specific type of beta-receptor in the lungs, and therefore have fewer side effects. These drugs come in both short-acting and long-acting forms. People who find inhalers hard to use may use nebulized or oral beta-agonists. For acute attacks, nebulizers are commonly used, and in the emergency room or hospital the doctor may give an injection too.

Handheld beta-agonist inhalers are the most common drugs prescribed for asthma. Examples include albuterol (trade names, Ventolin or Proventil). The short-acting form is the first-line agent for treatment of an acute attack. The newer long-acting forms can be used daily to prevent attacks and at bedtime by people who tend to have nocturnal attacks. Both the short- and long-acting forms can be used to prevent an attack before exposure to a known trigger. For example, people with exercise-induced asthma might use a beta-agonist inhaler before gym class, someone whose asthma is triggered by cold air might use an inhaler before ice skating, and a person with an allergy to cats might use an inhaler before visiting a friend who has a cat. The long-acting forms cannot be used for acute attacks, so if a person uses a long-acting beta-agonists to prevent exercise-induced bronchospasm, for example, they also need a short-acting agent for acute attacks.

The plus side is that beta-agonists are extremely effective in treating acute asthma attacks and are useful in preventing attacks brought on by known triggers. In addition, they have few side effects—only mild tremor, or shaking, of the hands and transient rapid heart rate. On the minus side, beta-agonists do not decrease the inflammation and hyperresponsiveness of asthmatic airways, and therefore, they do not change the course of asthma in the long run. Generally, they should be used only in combination with an anti-inflammatory agent, unless the person has very mild asthma.

Some researchers have blamed beta-agonists for the dramatic increase of severe and fatal asthma worldwide. Because the increase coincided with the increased use of beta-agonists, these researchers suggested that these drugs were the culprits—either because they were harmful, or because they were so effective in relieving asthma symptoms that people delayed seeking medical attention or stopped using other anti-inflammatory drugs. However, recent studies have suggested that the regular use of beta-agonists does not lead to less overall asthma control.

Anticholinergics

Anticholinergics are another type of drug designed to stop the body's mechanisms from doing something that causes problems. The beta-agonists work to activate cell receptors, while the anticholinergics block certain receptors. The nerve cells of the body release a substance called acetylcholine, which acts on receptors on other cells called cholinergic receptors. These actions cause the muscles surrounding the airways to contract, resulting in bronchospasm. Anticholinergic drugs serve as a block by stopping the acetylcholine from reaching the acetylcholine receptors. So they reverse or prevent bronchospasm.

As early as the 1800s, drugs with anticholinergic action were used to treat asthma. Powders made from deadly nightshade or belladonna plants were inhaled or swallowed to treat asthma. While these powders had anticholinergic effects, they were poisonous in larger doses and caused severe side effects in lower doses. Current anticholinergic drugs are purified, low-dose, and have minimal side effects—only mild dry mouth and dry eyes. Doctors often prescribe anticholinergic inhalers, and nebulized anticholinergics are used in hospitals in combination with a nebulized beta-agonist. These drugs are still relatively new and further long-term studies of their use in asthma are required.

Methylxanthines

Coffee or cola may improve asthma symptoms for some people. The caffeine in these drinks is a type of methylxanthine that has long been known to help some people with asthma. Synthetic methylxanthines (for example, theophylline) are available in oral and intravenous forms, but inhaled methylxanthine acts as an irritant and may actually cause bronchospasm. The mechanism of these drugs is still not clearly understood, but we know they relax smooth muscle in the airways and may also have some anti-inflammatory effect. However, they have not been found to decrease hyperresponsiveness with long-term use.

Methylxanthines may cause agitation, headache, nausea, and learning and behavioral problems, and if drug levels become too high, they can also cause convulsions and irregular heartbeat. These drugs are thought to be less powerful bronchodilators than beta-agonists, and they have some serious side effects, even if the dose is just a little too high. Usually the methylxanthines are used only for people with difficult-to-control asthma. People who are taking methylxanthines should be monitored with occasional blood tests to check drug levels and should check with their doctor before taking any other drugs.

Methylxanthines were once the most common drugs prescribed for asthma. As newer drugs with less toxic effects became available, the use of methylxanthines decreased. Now interest in methylxanthines is growing again, since they do have an anti-inflammatory effect.

Alternative Treatments

In addition to medications, many other treatments are used to try to control asthma symptoms. Some of these treatments may work for individual people with asthma, but few of them have been scientifically evaluated for effectiveness and safety.

Desensitization/Immunotherapy

Some people with allergies to specific substances get "allergy shots." Through a regular series of increasing doses of a substance they become "desensitized" and their bodies no longer react to the allergen. People with atopic asthma would seem to be ideal candidates for such a program, but attempts to desensitize asthma patients have been disappointing. Some patients improve after immunotherapy. Others actually worsen, with increased airway hyperreactivity. Research is continuing in this area. Immunotherapy

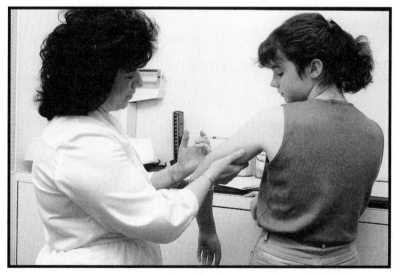

Allergy shots may sometimes improve symptoms of asthma.

is now only considered for asthma patients with proven allergic components, when environmental controls have not been effective and drug treatments have not controlled their symptoms.[1]

Breathing Exercises and Chest Physiotherapy

Anxiety can make many diseases worse, but in asthma it can be particularly troublesome. When people become anxious they often breathe rapidly—which can dry out the airways and decrease the amount of time available to exhale air through the narrowed airways. Learning how to breathe slowly and deeply, even during an asthma attack, by practicing deep breathing exercises may help some people. Chest physiotherapy is a technique used to help dislodge mucus and secretions from the lungs, and it can help if mucus is plugging the airways. It sounds like a medical procedure, but it consists essentially of pounding on the back to knock mucus out of the small airways. Family members can learn how to do chest physiotherapy to help people with asthma.

Over-the-Counter Medications

Many over-the-counter, or nonprescription, medications promise relief for asthma, but they can often be dangerous. Some nonprescription inhalers contain epinephrine or other substances that can relieve bronchospasm, but these medications have no affect on inflammation in the long run. So the cycle of inflammation and bronchospasm continues. Cough medicines and antihistamines can treat the cough and congestion of asthma, but they have no effect on the underlying disease. These drugs may help manage some asthma symptoms, but they should never be used without a doctor's recommendation.

Acupuncture, Homeopathy, Herbalism, Nutrition, and Mind–Body Therapies

Alternative medical treatments have become popular and may produce dramatic effects for some people. However, it is important to use such treatments only along with traditional medical treatment.

In acupuncture, certain areas of the body are stimulated with needles to treat symptoms and diseases. Acupuncture has been used for centuries in Asia. For the treatment of asthma, the "Din Chuan" point in the back has been shown to produce some improvement in symptoms in some studies.

Homeopathy is a method in which very low doses of the disease-causing agent, or an agent that causes similar symptoms, are thought to be capable of curing the disease—"like cures like." This treatment, in the case of asthma, is similar to immunotherapy and may sometimes be beneficial. However, like immunotherapy, it can also be dangerous, causing severe asthma attacks.

Some herbal medications claim to cure or treat asthma—and some may have anti-inflammatory or bronchodilatory effects. However, they may also contain harmful substances, so great care should be taken when using herbal medication. Some groups advocate nutritional therapies to control asthma—for example, high doses of vitamins C or B, magnesium, or fish oils. No scientific studies have shown the benefit of any of these nutritional strategies.

Yoga and hypnotherapy have also been used to try to control asthma attacks. The belief is that with training, the mind can control all aspects of the body's functioning—including bronchospasm and inflammation. In some cases, these techniques are effective. They can decrease stress levels and help control emotional factors that may be contributing to the symptoms.[2]

Because none of these techniques has been studied in any organized scientific way, it is difficult to know if they are harmful or beneficial. Before beginning any alternative treatment, people with asthma should discuss the situation with their doctors. They need to be sure the new treatment will not interfere with their present treatment, and that it is an appropriate treatment for their particular type of asthma. Doctors may also be able to recommend practitioners of alternative medicine who are well trained, responsible, and experienced in the treatment of asthma.

Some people with asthma find that yoga offers relief.

CHAPTER 7

Managing Asthma

The number of medications and types of treatments available for asthma seems enormous and may be confusing. Doctors often say that the more treatments we have for a disease, the further we are from a cure. Although this may be true to some extent, the treatments we have for asthma today are very effective. With appropriate management, people with asthma can live good, active lives.

Every person with asthma should be carefully examined, and the patient and doctor need to work out an individual plan of treatment together, with an emphasis on controlling the underlying inflammation as well as the symptoms. The plan should be reevaluated frequently. A person's asthma will change repeatedly, depending on environment, activities, and treatments. Even when the asthma seems to be under control, monitoring and treatment should be continued.

Choosing a Maintenance Regimen

After the initial diagnosis of asthma is made, the doctor will look at the pattern of asthma and, together with the patient, identify the apparent triggers. The asthma diary is an important information source for this evaluation. In some situations, a doctor may decide skin testing is needed to identify triggers. The next step in management is to begin trying to avoid or control exposures to triggers and irritants.

The doctor also evaluates the severity of the patient's asthma. Asthma is now usually divided into four categories: mild intermittent, mild persistent, moderate persistent, and severe persistent. Mild intermittent asthma means that the patient has fewer than two brief attacks of bronchospasm per week, with normal lung function between attacks and rare nocturnal symptoms. Mild persistent asthma

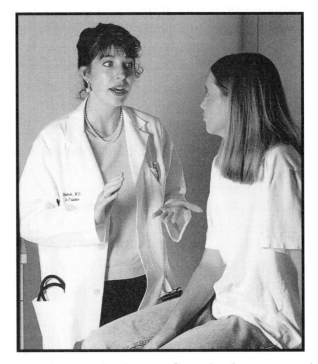

Asthma requires monitoring, and continuing communication with a doctor is crucial.

consists of more than two but fewer than seven attacks per week, or persistent mild symptoms, such as coughing or slight wheezing. In moderate persistent asthma, symptoms occur daily and nocturnal symptoms are more frequent or severe. Frequent severe attacks, daily symptoms, and lung function that may not return to normal between attacks characterize severe persistent asthma.

In mild intermittent asthma, the person's life is not greatly affected, so the goal of treatment is prompt relief from attacks. It can usually be controlled by avoiding triggers and using inhaled bronchodilators—such as a beta-agonist—for acute attacks and before exposure to known triggers such as exercise, cold air, or a furry creature. For mild persistent asthma, an anti-inflammatory agent should be used daily, in addition to bronchodilators when symptoms develop. For children, cromones are often the preferred anti-inflammatory agents, since they are generally effective and have minimal side effects. In adults, and in children whose attacks are not adequately controlled, inhaled steroids are the anti-inflammatory agent of choice. Cromones and inhaled steroids are only effective after several weeks of regular use. The anti-leukotrienes may also help these patients and may reduce steroid use.

In moderate or severe persistent asthma, a potent anti-inflammatory agent is essential, in addition to a bronchodilator. Inhaled steroids may be effective, and, especially in children, they are preferred to oral steroids because they have fewer side effects. However, if inhaled steroids do not control the asthma, a course of oral steroid therapy may be necessary. Additional medications are used as needed to control the symptoms. Having a home nebulizer may help patients with severe asthma avoid frequent visits to the emergency room.

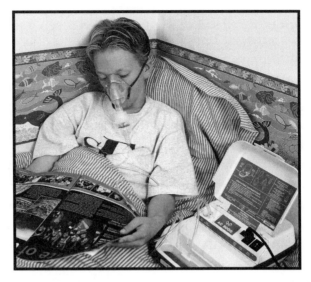

A patient breathes into the face mask of a home nebulizer to relieve asthma symptoms.

With any regimen, the most important instruction is to take the anti-inflammatory medications regularly—whether symptoms are present or not. Remember that even when a person with asthma is not wheezing or coughing or short of breath, a smoldering inflammatory response may be at work in their lungs, and if that person stops taking anti-inflammatory medication, the asthma may act up again. People use all sorts of memory helpers to remind themselves to take their medication, such as:

1. Take the medicine at the same time as another daily routine, such as brushing teeth or eating a meal.
2. Put a reminder on the bathroom mirror or on the refrigerator.
3. Use a one-day-at-a-time calendar, and rip off the page after taking the medicine.
4. Ask family members, friends, or teachers for reminders.

Making Asthma Regimens Dynamic and Flexible

Once a treatment regimen has been established, that is not the end of the story. Asthma is a changing condition and the therapy should be adjusted so that symptoms are controlled with the least amount of medication. For many reasons, asthma may become more—or less—severe. For example, as treatment is begun, and inflammation is reduced, severe asthma may become more controlled and it may be possible to stop some medications. Or as the pollen count rises, previously mild asthma can become more severe, and new medications may be needed. Or a person with asthma may become careless and use an inhaler incorrectly or forget doses of medication, leading to deterioration in that person's condition.

One way to judge how well a treatment plan is working is to count the number of attacks per week. Another way is to use peak flow meters to measure how well air moves through the airways. To use a peak flow meter, the person with asthma inhales deeply and then blows out as quickly and forcefully as possible through the meter. A scale on the device measures the peak expiratory flow in liters per minute. The normal peak flow rate varies with age, height, and sex, and fluctuates throughout the day. Normally the peak flow is higher at bedtime than in the morning. However, the difference between the morning and evening readings should be less than 20 percent. If the difference is 20 percent or more, it may indicate that the asthma is not well controlled or that an attack is imminent.

Peak flow measurements get lower before symptoms begin, so monitoring peak flow measurements may provide information on the asthma condition and can be used to

A peak flow meter measures current lung function.

guide medication adjustments. People who use peak flow meters should be given guidelines as to what their normal readings are, what their personal best is, and at what point they should adjust their medication, see their doctor, or go to the emergency room. These guidelines are called an "action plan."

Acute Asthma Attacks

Even when asthma is well controlled, an acute severe attack is possible, so every person with asthma should have a plan of action for acute attacks, in addition to a regular treatment regimen. Acute asthma attacks range from mild wheezing to severe shortness of breath. Rapid treatment is important to prevent worsening of the situation. The inflammation and bronchoconstriction in an acute attack feeds on itself. If it is not treated, it can set off a spiraling cascade of deteriorating function.

Home Treatment

Many people get warning signs that an asthma attack is coming. They may see a decrease in their peak flow readings, have a cough, or notice chest tightness or shortness of breath. Or they may simply feel tired or restless. When these warning signs occur, the first thing to do is to keep calm. Some people find that listening to music, watching television, or resting in a quiet room helps them stay calm. Relaxation techniques such as breathing exercises or yoga may help some people. At the same time, they can check their action plan to see what their next step should be.

Acute mild asthma is usually treated with inhaled bronchodilators—especially the fast-acting beta-agonists. Sometimes doctors prescribe home-nebulizer machines to use in an acute attack. If the attack does not pass or significantly improve after using a bronchodilator, a doctor should be contacted. In some situations the doctor may recommend starting an oral steroid or may want the patient to go to the doctor's office or emergency room. A person with asthma should also go to the emergency room if:

1. The peak flow continues to drop after using a bronchodilator.
2. The person is short of breath, and their neck or chest is pulled in with each breath.
3. The person has difficulty talking or walking.
4. The person has blue lips or fingernails, which would indicate that the oxygen level in the blood is low.

In the Emergency Room and the Hospital

If a trip to the emergency room is necessary, again the first thing to remember is to stay calm. If possible, a friend or family member should accompany the person with asthma. If there is time, a portable radio or a personal CD or cassette player might come in handy as a distraction. In the emergency room it is essential that people with asthma immediately identify themselves as someone having an acute attack so that treatment can be started quickly. Emergency rooms are often crowded, frenetic places. People with asthma attacks often look well from a distance or to an untrained observer, so they may be overlooked in the chaos of an emergency room. Speak up!

Initial treatment in the emergency room usually consists of giving oxygen and nebulized bronchodilators. Oxygen relieves some of the breathlessness and acts directly on the airways as a bronchodilator. A physical exam and peak flow measurements will be done to determine the severity of the attack. Sometimes an X ray of the chest is ordered to check for pneumonia, especially if the person has a fever or a cough.

The doctor may also want to do blood tests. This is done to look for evidence of infection or to check medication levels. A special blood test called an arterial blood gas (ABG) may be performed to measure the amounts of oxygen and carbon dioxide in the blood. This reflects how effectively a person is breathing. The doctor or nurse uses a small needle to take blood from an artery, usually in the wrist. Taking blood from an artery hurts more than the taking blood from a vein because the artery is deeper and surrounded by more muscle, but arterial blood gives the doctor the needed information. And the test is usually very quick.

If the bronchospasm does not improve promptly with bronchodilators and oxygen, or if the person is in severe distress, additional treatments are begun. An intravenous line may be started—a needle is inserted into a vein in the arm—so that intravenous steroids, and sometimes methylxanthines, can be given. Epinephrine and beta-agonists may be injected under the skin. These drugs usually cause some nervousness or agitation—on top of whatever the person is probably already feeling. This might be another good time to try some relaxation techniques, such as deep breathing or listening to music. If the attack does not improve in the emergency room, the person with asthma is admitted to the hospital for a longer course of nebulized bronchodilators and intravenous steroids (and antibiotics if bronchitis or pneumonia is also present).

When asthma is severe, the person may be unable to breathe in enough oxygen. Breathing through tightly constricted airways can be too hard and the person may become exhausted. In this situation, he or she may need temporary mechanical assistance to continue breathing. Ventilators are machines that take over the work of breathing until the airway inflammation and bronchoconstriction improve. When a ventilator is needed, the doctor inserts a tube through the person's nose or mouth into the lungs so that the machine can deliver oxygen to the lungs and remove carbon dioxide. This "intubation" procedure is uncomfortable and can be scary. A local anesthetic is applied to the nose or throat, and calming medication may be given. It is not always possible to put the patient to sleep for this procedure because of the urgency of the situation, and because sedation may decrease the person's basic drive to breathe and worsen the situation. However, mechanical ventilation can be a life-saving procedure.

While on the ventilator, the person with asthma can rest. The doctors may prescribe calming medication to make the patient more comfortable. Meanwhile, the patient receives high doses of bronchodilators and steroids to treat the asthma. Once the bronchoconstriction has resolved, the breathing tube is removed and the patient is able to breathe on his or her own. Usually the tube is removed within a few days.

After the acute asthma attack is over, whether hospitalization was required or not, the patient's maintenance regimen and action plans should be reevaluated. The person with asthma may need more instruction in the proper use of inhalers or may need a spacer device. Maybe a higher-dose anti-inflammatory agent is required. Sometimes the trigger of the attack was an infection, a new pet in the house, smoking a cigarette, or playing a game of soccer. In these cases, the doctor might advise ways to avoid or manage triggers. By reviewing the symptoms in the days before the attack, the person with asthma may be able to learn what his or her warning signs are for an asthma attack and make a new action plan.

Remember that the management of asthma is an on-going cooperative effort between the person with asthma and the doctor. Asthma is still a lifelong condition and requires constant attention.

Living with Asthma

Poorly treated asthma can be a life-threatening disease. But when asthma is treated properly, people can live a normal life free of any symptoms or limitations. Throughout history, people with asthma have been able to live active and accomplished lives—even before today's improved treatments were available.

Several U.S. presidents had asthma—including Theodore Roosevelt, Martin Van Buren, and Woodrow Wilson. The great musicians and composers Ludwig van Beethoven and Antonio Vivaldi suffered with it too. John Paul Jones, the naval hero of the American Revolution who faced overwhelming odds in battle with the statement, "I have not yet begun to fight," fought against severe asthma all his life. The revolutionary Che Guevara also had asthma.[1] And the list could go on for many pages.

Perhaps most striking is the number of successful athletes with asthma. In the 1984 Los Angeles Olympic Games, 67 of 596 U.S. athletes (11 percent) had asthma and 41 of them won medals—15 gold, 21 silver, and 5 bronze.[2] Well-known Olympic medalists with asthma include track star Jackie Joyner-Kersee, diver Greg Louganis, and swimmers

97

Tom Dolan and Nancy Hogshead. Hogshead, the 1984 Olympic gold medalist in swimming, spoke for all of them when she said: "Asthma does not stop me from what I want to do in life. I choose what I want to do. My asthma doesn't decide. The reason why it doesn't stop me is because I take good care of my asthma."[3]

Although asthma is still a lifelong condition, it can be controlled and managed. However, even with the appropriate medication and a near trigger-free environment, an asthma attack is always possible. People with asthma need to make some minimal adjustments to their lives and be prepared with an action plan for attacks.

Special Situations

Sports and Exercise

Many people with asthma—up to 90 percent of them—have symptoms when they exercise. But these symptoms do not mean they should limit their activity! Regular exercise can actually decrease the frequency and severity of attacks; it also improves self-confidence, physical well-being, and overall fitness.

However, people who have asthma should take precautions when they exercise. They should be sure to do some low-level exercises before beginning any rigorous activity. Cold air is particularly irritating to the airways, so if the day is cold a scarf over the mouth and nose can help warm the air before it enters the airways. On days with a high pollen count, indoor activities may be better, such as track, volleyball, or basketball. Swimming is also less irritating to the

Olympic athlete Jackie Joyner-Kersee uses an inhaler after a track competition to control her asthma.

airways, since the air is usually warm and humid. Cross-country skiing or ice skating may be inadvisable for people with severe asthma.

Using an inhaled beta-agonist or cromolyn from five to sixty minutes before exercise should help prevent bronchospasm. Teachers and coaches should be told that a child has exercise-induced bronchospasm, but they should also know that asthma is no limitation to activity. The Olympic Committee and other sports supervisory groups regulate certain drugs for athletes, because they may give an unfair advantage. These groups may ban some of the drugs used to treat asthma. The U.S. Olympic Committee provides a current list of approved medications for athletes (see For Further Information for a toll-free telephone number).

One sport that people with asthma should perhaps avoid is scuba diving. Scuba divers stay underwater for prolonged periods carrying tanks of air (*scuba* stands for self-contained underwater breathing apparatus). When scuba divers dive deep into the water, pressure builds up around them. This high pressure compresses the air inside their lungs, and as they breathe in more air from their tanks, the total amount of air in their lungs increases. Then as the divers come up to the surface, the pressure decreases, and the air inside their lungs expands.[4]

If they do not exhale the excess air, the lungs will expand—and if they expand too much, they can be damaged. The small air sacs in the lungs can burst, releasing air into the chest wall or the bloodstream. These bubbles in the bloodstream are called air emboli, and they can be dangerous, even fatal if they travel to the brain or another vital organ. Some people believe that people with asthma are more prone to this problem, since their narrowed airways may limit the release of excess air during their ascent to the surface. And, of course, if they suffered an asthma attack underwater, the situation would become even more dangerous.

School and Work

School can sometimes be a difficult place for children with asthma. They may be embarrassed to pull out an inhaler, or for people to hear them wheezing in class. Classrooms may have triggers such as carpeting, mold, chalk dust, paints, and chemicals. Other children may not understand what asthma is and may imagine that the condition is contagious. One thing to remember is that asthma is a very common illness—10 percent or more of the children in any school are likely to have asthma. And it is more embarrassing to have a severe asthma attack in school than it is to pull out an inhaler and take a couple of puffs.

Surgery and the Dentist

People with asthma should always tell their doctors and dentists about their condition before any surgery or other procedure is done. Major surgeries involving the heart or lungs are higher risk if asthma is not under good control. Sometimes surgery can be delayed until the asthma is better controlled. If the person has been on oral steroids prior to surgery, they may need an extra dose to prevent adrenal insufficiency during the stress of surgery.

Traveling

Whenever people with asthma travel, they should make sure to bring enough medication with them—including any supplies they might need for an acute attack. They can find out ahead of time about the climate of their destination. If pollens are a problem, the National Allergy Bureau has a hotline to call to find out about the pollen seasons around the world (see For Further Information). When reserving a hotel room, people with asthma can request

Smoking or being around smoke is dangerous for people wih asthma.

air-conditioning and nonsmoking rooms to reduce the risk that the room will trigger an attack.

Smoking, Drugs, and Alcohol

Smoking anything, or being around anyone who is smoking, is a powerful trigger for asthma. People with asthma should never smoke even one cigarette. Drugs and alcohol can also be a problem for people with asthma. Sometimes alcohol triggers attacks, and poor judgment caused by intoxication can be dangerous if an attack occurs.

Intimacy and Sex

Intimacy and sex can create concerns for people with asthma. Some people find that when they are physically close to a partner, they have an asthma attack. People with exercise-induced asthma may worry that intercourse will trigger an attack. These concerns are not unfounded. Sometimes a perfume, cologne, soap, or shampoo that a partner is using can trigger an attack, and sometimes the physical exertion of intercourse induces bronchospasm. More often, though, it is worry and anxiety that triggers the attack.

To deal with these potential problems, couples should discuss the situation. Asthma is nothing to be ashamed of, and it is certainly not a sign of weakness. Perfumed products can be avoided, and using a bronchodilator before intercourse, just as before any other physical activity, can also help. If problems persist, a doctor may be able to make other suggestions.

Pregnancy and Breast-Feeding

When a woman with asthma becomes pregnant, the disease takes on a new dimension. It is no longer just the woman's problem—now it is a condition that can affect the fetus as well. The fetus receives oxygen from the mother's bloodstream. If the mother's asthma is not well controlled, the fetus may not get enough oxygen, which can lead to low birthweight and premature delivery. The woman is also put at risk in this situation, with a higher risk of complicated labor, high blood pressure, and a condition called preeclampsia, which can lead to seizures.

About one-third of women with asthma improve during pregnancy, one-third get worse, and one-third remain the same. Sometimes asthma is first diagnosed during pregnancy. Changes that occur in the body during pregnancy often make women feel short of breath. This may be normal, but it may also be the first sign of asthma or indicate an asthma attack in a woman who has asthma.

Asthma management during pregnancy is really no different from management at other times—except that the stakes are higher—so closer monitoring of symptoms and strict avoidance of triggers is required. Most of the medications used for asthma are thought to be relatively safe in pregnancy. And uncontrolled asthma is a greater risk to both the woman and the fetus than are any of the asthma medications.

When attacks do occur, early action can reduce the likelihood of the episode progressing to a severe attack. Pregnant women should quickly seek medical help for an acute attack if their home action plan is not rapidly successful. In the third trimester, the woman may be instructed to seek medical care at the first sign of an attack so that the fetus can be monitored.

Asthma attacks during pregnancy are often associated with uterine contractions that usually do not progress to labor and stop when the asthma attack is over. When a pregnant woman with asthma is admitted to the hospital in labor she should tell the staff about her condition so that appropriate measures can be taken. Over-the-counter medications such as decongestants and primatene mist are not recommended during pregnancy.

When asthma is properly controlled, women with asthma can have normal pregnancies with little or no increased risk. After the baby is born, there is no reason that the woman with asthma should not breast-feed. Nearly all medications enter the breast milk, but the levels are very low, so most of these medications can be used while breast-feeding.[5]

CHAPTER 9

The Future

Will we ever find a cure for asthma? Looking at the record, you might be doubtful. Asthma has been recognized for more than 3,000 years and we have not discovered its cause yet, let alone developed a cure. We even quibble over the definition of asthma. However, over the last fifty years, research in the field of immunology has progressed rapidly. We have been able to understand and outline the many steps in the development of asthma, even if we still do not know the underlying cause. And many new approaches to treating asthma are under development. Some of the most promising lines of research are:

1. Synthetic inactive antibodies that could block the binding sites of IgE
2. Techniques to make the TH2 (type 2 helper) cells unresponsive to stimulation or to direct the immune response to the **TH1** (type 1 helper) pathway instead of the TH2 pathway
3. Gene therapy to replace the abnormal genes in people with asthma with normal genes
4. Genetic screening followed by strict avoidance of

exposure to allergens in individuals found to be genetically predisposed to develop asthma

5. Specific antagonists to some of the chemicals released by the immune cells involved in the inflammatory cascade causing asthma.

Can you think of some other ideas?

Another more immediate challenge for the future is trying to explain and control the epidemic of asthma in inner-city areas. Several educational programs have been started in an effort to reduce the severity of asthma in these areas. Much of the problem is related to poor health care and ignorance of the need to treat asthma as a chronic disease, so education should go a long way in improving the situation. The other part of the problem in these areas is the unhealthy living conditions—air pollution, crowding, damp and dirty buildings with poor ventilation, and rodent and insect infestations. These issues are more difficult to solve, but the advantages would be enormous in terms of decreasing the incidence and severity of asthma.

Despite the difficulties in finding a cure for asthma and the increasing rates of asthma throughout the world, people with asthma can live normal lives. Proper care, a good asthma regimen, and avoidance of as many triggers as possible can control the symptoms of asthma. If you have asthma, take good care of yourself with proper nutrition, exercise, and rest. Stress reduction can help. Finding support from family, friends, school, or support groups will improve your health and well-being even more. Asthma may be a lifelong condition, but you can still have a long— and full—life.

With proper attention and medical care, asthma sufferers can lead normal lives.

Introduction

1. John Carpi, "Olympian Swims by Exercise-Induced Asthma," *Internal Medicine News*, September 1, 1996.
2. Jere Longman, "U.S. Earns First Gold in the Pool," *New York Times*, July 22, 1996.

Chapter One

1. Alex Sakula, "A History of Asthma," *Journal of the Royal College of Physicians of London*, 1988, vol. 22, no. 1: 36–44.
2. Sheldon G. Cohen, "Asthma in Antiquity: The Ebers Papyrus," *Allergy and Asthma Proceedings*, 1992, vol. 13, no. 3: 147–154.
3. Hippocrates, *The Genuine Works of Hippocrates*, trans. F. Adams, (Baltimore: Williams & Wilkins, 1939).
4. Aretaeus, *The Extant Words of Aretaeus, the Cappadocian*, trans. F. Adams, (London: Sydenham Society, 1856).
5. Moses Maimonides, *Treatise on Asthma*, edited by S. Muntner, (Philadelphia: Lippincott, 1963).

Chapter Two

Gary L. Larson, "Asthma in Children," *New England Journal of Medicine*, 1992, vol. 326, no. 23: 1540–1545, and E. R. McFadden Jr. and I. A. Gilbert, "Asthma,"*New England Journal of Medicine*, 1992, vol. 327, no. 27: 1928–1937, were used as general references.

Chapter Three

1. U.S. statistical data from the National Center for Health Statistics, United States Vital Records.
2. National Institutes of Health, National Heart, Lung, and Blood Institute, *Global Initiative for Asthma*, NIH publication no. 95–3659, 1995.
3. A. Sandford, T. Weir, and P. Pare, "The Genetics of Asthma," *American Journal of Respiratory and Critical Care Medicine*, 1996, vol. 153: 1749–1765.
4. J. Morris, "Experiences and Findings of a Medical Officer on Tristan da Cunha, February 1994–February 1995," *South African Medical Journal*, 1997, vol. 87: 323–327.
5. N. Zamel, et al. "Asthma on Tristan da Cunha: Looking for the Genetic Link," *American Journal of Respiratory and Critical Care Medicine*, 1996, vol. 153: 1902–1906.
6. D. S. Postma, et al. "Genetic Susceptibility to Asthma-Bronchial Hyperresponsiveness Coinherited with a Major Gene for Atopy," *New England Journal of Medicine*, 1995, vol. 333: 894–900.
7. Center for Disease Control, *Asthma—United States, 1980–1990.*
8. E. F. Crain, K. B. Weiss, et al., "An Estimate of the Prevalence of Asthma and Wheezing among Inter-City Children" *Pediatrics*, 1994, vol. 94: 356–362.

Chapter Four

1. U.S. statistical data from the National Center for Health Statistics, United States Vital Records.
2. L. Claudio, et al., "Socioeconomic Factors and Asthma Hospitalization Rates in New York City," *Journal of Asthma*, 1999, vol. 36: 343–350.

3. K. B. Weiss and D. K. Wagener, "Changing Patterns of Asthma Mortality," *Journal of the American Medical Association,* 1990, vol. 264: 1683–1720.

Chapter Five

1. D. L. Rosenstreich, et al., "The Role of Cockroach Allergy and Exposure to Cockroach Allergen in Causing Morbidity among Inner-City Children with Asthma," *New England Journal of Medicine,* 1997, vol. 336: 1356–1363.
2. Pam Belluck, "As Asthma Cases Rise, Tough Choices and Lessons," *New York Times,* September 29, 1996.
3. W. M. Busse, et al., "Stress and Asthma," *American Journal of Respiratory and Critical Care Medicine,* 1995, vol. 151: 249–252.
4. E. Goode, "Can an Essay a Day Keep Asthma at Bay?" *New York Times,* April 14, 1999.

Chapter Six

1. P. S. Norman and P. J. Barnes, "Is There a Role for Immunotherapy in the Treatment of Asthma?" *American Journal of Respiratory and Critical Care Medicine,* 1996, vol. 154: 1225–1228.
2. G. T. Lewith and A. D. Watkins, "Unconventional Therapies in Asthma: An Overview," *Allergy* 1996, vol. 51: 761–769.

Chapter Seven

National Institutes of Health *Expert Panel Report 2: Guidelines for the Diagnosis and Management of Asthma,* National Heart, Lung, and Blood Institute, 1997, was used as a general reference.

Chapter Eight

1. *Allergy and Asthma Proceedings* (recurring series) "Asthma in History."
2. R. O. Voy, "U.S. Olympic Committee Experience with Exercise-Induced Bronchospasm," *Medical Science Sports Exercise,* 1986, vol. 18: 328–330.
3. Carpi, "Olympian Swims."
4. H. M. Schanker and S. L. Spector, "Scuba Diving in Individuals with Asthma," *Allergy and Asthma Proceedings,* 1996, vol. 17: 311–313.
5. National Asthma Education Program, *Report of the Working Group on Asthma and Pregnancy,* National Institutes of Health, National Heart, Lung, and Blood Institute, NIH Publication no. 93–3279A, March 1993.

allergen—a substance that can cause an allergic reaction

allergy—a condition in which the immune system reacts abnormally to allergens

alveoli—small sacs in the lungs where oxygen is exchanged for carbon dioxide

anaphylaxis—an extreme allergic reaction in which the airways constrict and there is a severe shortness of breath

antibodies—proteins produced by B-lymphocytes that interact with a particular molecule, or antigen; each antibody is a specific match for a specific antigen

antigen—a substance that can produce a response by the immune system; antigens may be parts of bacteria or viruses, toxins, or particulate matter

antigen presenting cell—a cell that takes up foreign particles and processes them; the cell then presents a portion of the foreign particle—the antigenic part—on its surface in a form recognizable to other cells so that the immune system can defend against the invader

anti-leukotrienes—drugs that block or prevent the production of substances called leukotrienes, which are produced by many of the body's white blood cells

asthma—a chronic disease of the respiratory system, characterized by inflammation of the airways and episodic shortness of breath caused by narrowing of the airways

atopic—tending to develop allergic reactions to common substances

B-cells or B-lymphocytes—cells of the immune system produced in the bone marrow and released into the bloodstream; they are distinguished by their ability to produce antibodies

beta-agonists—drugs that stimulate the beta-receptors, causing relaxation of smooth muscles and dilation of the airways

bronchi—larger air passages of the lungs

bronchoconstriction—narrowing of the bronchi, or airways, usually caused by contraction of the smooth muscles surrounding the airways—a major symptom of asthma

bronchospasm—sudden or spasmodic bronchoconstriction caused by contraction of the smooth muscles surrounding the airways

chemotaxis—the movement of a cell in response to chemical substances; various cells of the immune system are attracted to sites of inflammation by this process

cilia—tiny hairlike projections on the surface of cells which propel the cell or move fluid over the cell surface; on the tracheobronchial tree, they move in waves to sweep mucus and foreign particles out of the respiratory system

cromones—drugs that inhibit the release of histamine and other substances from mast cells

cytokines—proteins released by various cells of the immune system; they communicate information to other cells

cytotoxic—poisonous or deadly to a cell

dander—small particles of skin, hair, or feathers of animals that can cause allergic reactions in sensitive people

eosinophils—white blood cells that play a role in allergic reactions and asthma, releasing histamine and leukotrienes

hyperresponsive or hyperreactive—prone to overreact in response to stimuli; in asthma, the term refers to the tendency of the airways to constrict rapidly in response to various stimuli

IgE (immunoglobulin E)—a class of antibody important in allergy; it binds to specific receptors on eosinophils and mast cells and triggers the release of substances that cause an allergic response

incidence—the number of people who develop a disorder in a given period of time, usually expressed as a percentage of the population

inflammation—a local protective response after injury to body tissues; characterized by pain, heat, swelling, and loss of function of the involved area

leukocytes—blood cells that fight infection; also called white blood cells

leukotrienes—substances that are released by white blood cells and cause various reactions; in asthma, they cause bronchoconstriction, dilation of blood vessels, and chemotaxis of inflammatory cells

lymphocytes—leukocytes responsible for specific immune responses; they include B-cells and T-cells

macrophages—leukocytes specialized to eat or engulf and digest foreign particles; they also act as antigen presenting cells and produce multiple substances important in the immune response

mast cell—a cell capable of releasing multiple substances, including histamine, which are important in inflammation and in allergic reactions

mortality—the number of deaths due to a particular disease or condition

pathogens—disease-causing agents

phagocytes—cells capable of the ingestion of particulate matter

pulmonary—involving the lungs

steroids—drugs that systemically decrease the immune response

T-cells or T-lymphocytes—white blood cells processed in the thymus before being released into the bloodstream; in the immune system response, they signal other cells to attack invaders and control the antibody production of B-cells

TH1 and TH2 cells—subtypes of helper T-cells; the TH1 (type 1 helper) cells stimulate a normal protective immune response; the TH2 (type 2 helper) cells set in motion the cascade of reactions that produce an allergic reaction

wheezing—the high-pitched sound produced when air moves through narrowed airways

white blood cells—cells in the blood that fight infection; also called leukocytes

Books

Adams, Francis V. *The Asthma Sourcebook: Everything You Need to Know.* Los Angeles: Lowell House, 1995.

American Medical Association, ed., *Essential Guide to Asthma.* New York: Pocket Books, 2000.

Edelman, Norman H. *The American Lung Association's Family Guide to Asthma and Allergies.* Boston: Little, Brown, 1997.

Edelson, Edward. *Allergies.* New York: Chelsea House Publishers, 1989.

Murphy, Wendy B. *Asthma.* Brookfield, CT: Millbrook Press, 1997.

Silverstein, Alvin, Virginia Silverstein, and Laura Silverstein Nunn. *Asthma.* Springfield, NJ: Enslow Publishers, 1997.

Simpson, Carolyn. *Coping with Asthma.* New York: Rosen Publishing Group, 1995.

Information Lines

These toll-free numbers provide recorded information about asthma.

Lung Facts
National Jewish Medical and Research Center
(800) 552-LUNG
For information about asthma and allergies

National Allergy Bureau
(800) 9POLLEN
For local pollen count information and helpful hints on asthma

U.S. Olympic Committee's Olympic Drug Reference Line
(800) 233-0393
For information about the status of a medication

Organizations

Any of the following organizations can provide more information about asthma. They can be contacted through the mail, on the telephone, or on the Web.

Allergy and Asthma Network/Mothers of Asthmatics, Inc.
3554 Chain Bridge Road, Suite 200
Fairfax, VA 22030
(800) 878-4403
http://www.aanma.org

American Academy of Allergy, Asthma and Immunology
611 East Wells Street
Milwaukee, WI 53202
(800) 822-2762
http://wwaaaai.org

American College of Allergy, Asthma and Immunology
800 East Northwest Highway, Suite 1080
Palatine, IL 60067
(800) 842-7777
http://allergy.mcg.org/

American Lung Association
1740 Broadway
New York, NY 10019
(212) 315-8700
(800) 586-4872
http://www.lungusa.org

Asthma and Allergy Foundation of America
1125 15th Street NW, Suite 502
Washington, DC 20005
(202) 466-7643
(800) 7ASTHMA
http:///www.aafa.org

Canadian Lung Association
1900 City Park Drive, Suite 508
Blair Business Park
Gloucester, Ontario K1J 1A3
Canada
(613) 747-6776
(888) 566-LUNG in Canada
http://www.lung.ca/asthma/

National Asthma Education and Prevention Program
National Heart, Lung, and Blood Institute
Information Center
P.O. Box 30105
Bethesda, MD 20824-0105
(301) 592-8573
http://www.nhlbi.nih.gov/about/naepp/index.htm

INDEX

Alissa Greenberg, a graduate of Yale University, earned her medical degree from Columbia University. She completed her residency in internal medicine at Columbia Presbyterian Medical Center in New York City and her fellowship in pulmonary and critical care medicine at New York University Medical Center. Dr. Greenberg is now on the faculty of the New York University School of Medicine.